THE BOOK OF

Chocolates & Petits Fours

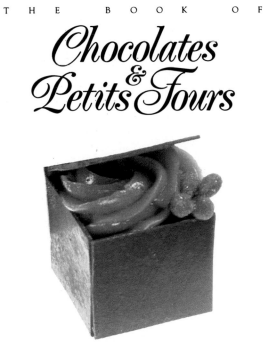

THE BOOK OF

Chocolates & Petits Fours

BEVERLEY SUTHERLAND SMITH

Photography by
PHILIP WYMANT

TED SMART

This edition produced for
The Book People
Hall Wood Avenue
Haydock
St Helens WA11 9OL

By arrangement with Merehurst Fairfax,
51–57 Lacy Road, Putney, London SW15 1PR

ISBN 1 85613 915 8

Editors: Susan Tomnay, Chris Fayers
Designers: Susan Kinealy, Roger Daniels, Richard Slater, Stuart Willard
Food stylist: Beverley Sutherland Smith
Photographer: Philip Wymant
Typeset by Lineage
Colour separation by Fotographics Ltd, London–Hong Kong
Printed and bound in Spain by Bookprint, S.L.

Notes:
All spoon measurements are equal.
1 teaspoon = 5 ml spoon.
1 tablespoon = 15 ml spoon.

Contents

Introduction

Petits fours are tiny biscuits and iced cakes served at the end of a meal usually with a cup of coffee. One of the greatest French chefs of the eighteenth century, Carême, said that these little cakes were baked in the oven after the large cakes had been removed and the oven had cooled slightly. These after dinner delights extend now to include small fancy biscuits, tiny tarts and confectionery, such as chocolate coated fruits, marzipan sweets and nut confections. There has also been an increase of interest in exquisitely moulded chocolates to serve after dinner, but there is an added charm in the individual texture and taste which shows in produce which is homemade, even if not as perfect as commercial in appearance. This book has a wide collection of chocolates, petits fours and other confections which I think are especially delicious and vary from those which can be made very quickly to others requiring more time for special occasions. When assembling this collection, I felt it really important that they could be made without the necessity of sweetmaking or chocolate equipment, such as moulds, and were not beyond the ability of most home cooks. Not only can these be served after dinner, but many of them make ideal gifts. They are all delicious – the ultimate indulgence after a meal.

Fruity Chocolates

155g (5 oz) plain (dark) chocolate, chopped
60g (2 oz/⅓ cup) finely chopped glacé cherries
1 tablespoon finely chopped glacé ginger
3 tablespoons finely chopped glacé pineapple
1 tablespoon finely chopped glacé apricots
2 teaspoons orange liqueur

TO DECORATE: 24 almond flakes

Melt 90g (3 oz) chocolate in a bowl or top of a double boiler set over a pan of simmering water. Drop 24 small chocolate rounds by teaspoon on greaseproof paper and flatten. Let set.

Mix fruit with liqueur. Let stand for 30 minutes. Using about ½ tablespoon form fruit mixture into small balls and press to same diameter as chocolate rounds. Place flattened fruit on top of each chocolate round.

To decorate, melt remaining 65g (2 oz) chocolate in a bowl or top of a double boiler set over a pan of simmering water. Spoon chocolate into a small pastry bag fitted with a small plain writing tip. Pipe a lattice design on top of each fruity chocolate. Place an almond flake on top of each. Let set. Store layered with greaseproof paper, in an airtight container up to 3 weeks.

Makes 24 chocolates.

Chocolate Fruit Crisps

125g (4 oz) plain (dark) chocolate, chopped
90g (3 oz/¾ cup) stoned dates, finely chopped
60g (2 oz/½ cup) pecans, finely chopped
90g (3 oz/⅓ cup) caster sugar
90g (3 oz/⅓ cup) butter
30g (1 oz/1 cup) rice breakfast cereal
45g (1½ oz/½ cup) coconut

Line a 27 x 18cm (11 x 7in) baking pan with foil; grease foil. Melt chocolate in a bowl or top of a double boiler set over a pan of simmering water. Stir until smooth. Spread over foil. Let chocolate partially set.

Heat dates, nuts, sugar and butter in a small saucepan until the butter is hot. Stir occasionally. Combine rice cereal and coconut in a large bowl. Stir in date mixture. Mix well. Spread on top of chocolate base. Spread and flatten mixture firmly so it holds together.

Chill until set. Invert and remove foil. Invert again so rice topping is uppermost. Cut what is needed into strips. Cover and store remainder in refrigerator up to 1 week.

Makes 40 pieces.

Chocolate-Coated Fruit

4 glacé pineapple halves
8 dried apricots
3 large glacé apricots or dried figs
220g (7 oz) milk or plain (dark) chocolate
2 teaspoons unflavoured vegetable oil

If dried apricots are very hard, cover with boiling water for 30 seconds. Drain well and pat dry with paper towel. Melt chocolate and oil in a bowl or top of a double boiler set over a pan of simmering water. Stir until smooth.

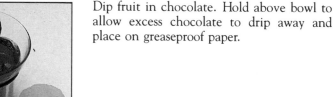

Dip fruit in chocolate. Hold above bowl to allow excess chocolate to drip away and place on greaseproof paper.

When cool, refrigerate in a covered container up to 2 weeks. Cut into pieces to expose a cross-section of colour, if desired.

Makes 15 pieces.

Dried Fruit Confections

60g (2 oz/¹⁄₃ cup) dried figs
250g (8 oz/1½ cups) dried apricots
125g (4 oz/2 cups) dried apples
125g (4 oz/1 cup) pecans or walnuts
185g (6 oz/¾ cup) caster sugar
185g (6 oz) white chocolate, chopped
30g (1 oz) butter

Place fruit in a medium bowl and cover with boiling water for 5 seconds; drain. Let stand 4 hours in covered bowl to soften fruit.

In a blender or food processor fitted with a steel blade, process fruit until texture is smooth. Add nuts and sugar and process until mixture is smooth. Spread fruit mixture evenly on greaseproof paper to a 30 x 20cm (12 x 8in) square. Smooth by using a knife dipped in hot water. Cover top with additional piece of greaseproof paper. Leave fruit in a cool place for 3 days to firm and dry slightly.

Melt chocolate and butter in a bowl or top of a double boiler set over a pan of simmering water. Stir until smooth. Remove greaseproof paper from top of fruit and spread ½ of chocolate over fruit in a thin layer. Stretch and place plastic wrap over chocolate while warm to produce a smooth finish. Let stand 3 minutes. Turn over carefully and remove greaseproof paper. Spread with remaining chocolate and press with plastic wrap. Refrigerate to set. When set, peel off plastic wrap. Cut into 60 small squares. Store in refrigerator up to 3 weeks.

Makes 60 pieces.

— Chocolate-Coated Orange Strips —

2 thick-skinned medium oranges, halved
250g (8 oz/1 cup) sugar
250 ml (8 fl oz/1 cup) water
125g (4 oz) plain (dark) chocolate, chopped

Squeeze juice from orange halves. Discard pieces of orange and membranes, but do not remove pith. Cut each orange skin into 10 strips, 1cm (½in) thick. Place peel in a medium saucepan, cover with cold water and bring to boil. Repeat procedure 4 times, cooking the last time until peel is translucent. Drain well.

Combine sugar and water in a medium saucepan and cook over low heat until sugar has dissolved. Increase heat to medium-high. Continue cooking for 1 minute. Add orange strips; cook until syrup is reduced, stirring occasionally. Reduce heat if liquid begins to cook away. Place in a single layer and dry orange strips on a wire rack set over a baking sheet for 24 hours.

Melt chocolate in a bowl or top of a double boiler set over a pan of simmering water. Dip half of each orange strip in chocolate. Cool on greaseproof paper. Let set at room temperature. Store in a covered container in refrigerator up to 2 weeks.

Makes 80 pieces.

—— Twice Dipped Strawberries ——

20 medium to large sized strawberries
60g (2 oz) plain (dark) chocolate, chopped
60g (2 oz) white chocolate, chopped

Melt plain chocolate in a bowl or top of a double boiler set over a pan of simmering water. Stir until smooth.

Insert a cocktail stick into green hull and dip end of strawberry into chocolate. Place on a wire rack with the hull downwards to set.

Melt white chocolate in a bowl or top of a double boiler set over a pan of simmering water. Stir until smooth. Holding green hull, dip plain chocolate end of the strawberry in white chocolate, leaving some of plain chocolate showing. Place on a wire rack with hull upwards to set. Chill several hours.

Makes 20 dipped strawberries.

Ginger & Date Pyramids

60g (2 oz/⅓ cup) glacé ginger, finely chopped
75g (2½ oz/½ cup) stoned dates, finely chopped
2 teaspoons brandy
90g (3 oz) plain (dark) chocolate, chopped

TO DECORATE: dessicated coconut

Mix ginger, dates and brandy in a small bowl and let stand 1 hour.

Form mixture into tiny pyramids and place on greaseproof paper. Chill for 1 hour or until firm.

Melt chocolate in a bowl or top of a double boiler set over a pan of simmering water. Stir until smooth. Spoon chocolate over top of each pyramid. To decorate, dust top lightly with coconut. Cool until firm. Store in an airtight container with paper between layers up to 3 weeks.

Makes 12 pyramids.

Apricots with Hazelnut Filling

9 to 12 medium dried apricots, halved
60g (2 oz/¹/₂ cup) hazelnuts
60g (2 oz/¹/₃ cup) icing sugar
2 teaspoons orange liqueur
1 egg white

TO COAT: 90g (3 oz) plain (dark) chocolate, chopped

Preheat oven to 180C (350F/Gas 4). In a small bowl, cover apricots with boiling water. Let stand 3 minutes. Drain and spread on paper towels to dry 1 hour. Roast hazelnuts on a baking sheet in preheated oven 10 minutes or until golden brown and skin has blistered. Wrap in a towel; let stand 5 minutes. Rub towel to remove skins. Grind nuts finely. To make filling, mix nuts with sugar, orange liqueur and sufficient egg white to form a moist paste.

Roll filling into small ovals the length of an apricot. Place filling on each apricot. Fold apricot over to enclose filling. Press apricot to make a neat shape, showing some filling. Chill 1 hour.

Melt chocolate in a bowl or top of a double boiler set over a pan of simmering water. Stir until smooth. Dip one or both ends of apricots in chocolate. Place on greaseproof paper until set. Refrigerate in a covered container with greaseproof paper between layers up to 10 days.

Makes 18 to 24 apricots.

Cherry Nut Chocolates

100g (3½ oz) plain (dark) chocolate, chopped
30g (1 oz/¼ cup) macadamia nuts or blanched
almonds, coarsely chopped
8 glacé cherries, quartered

Grate or chop chocolate.

Toast nuts in a dry frying pan until golden brown. Stir occasionally. Cool. Melt chocolate in a bowl or top of a double boiler set over a pan of simmering water. Stir until smooth. Drop by teaspoonfuls on greaseproof paper and flatten to form thick small buttons. Let partly set.

Sprinkle nuts on outside rim of chocolate. Press cherry piece in centre. Let set; peel from greaseproof paper. Refrigerate in a covered container with greaseproof paper between layers up to 3 weeks.

Makes 30 chocolates.

Walnut Coffee Creams

FILLING: 60 ml (2 fl oz/¼ cup) thick cream
2 teaspoons liquid glucose
1½ teaspoons instant coffee powder
90g (3 oz/½ cup) icing sugar
90g (3 oz) plain (dark) chocolate, chopped
40 walnut halves or large walnut pieces

In a small saucepan, cook cream and glucose over a low heat until glucose dissolves. Remove from heat; add coffee. Mix thoroughly; cool. Stir in sugar; mixture should form soft peaks. If not, add some additional sugar. Chill covered 2 hours.

Melt chocolate in a bowl or top of a double boiler set over a pan of simmering water. Stir until smooth. Drop by teaspoonfuls on greaseproof paper and flatten to form small chocolate buttons. Let set.

Spoon filling into a small pastry bag fitted with a fluted nozzle. Pipe a rosette around edge of each chocolate button. Leave indentation in centre. Place a walnut piece in cavity. Chill 30 minutes or until firm. Remove paper. Refrigerate in a covered container with greaseproof paper between layers up to 2 weeks.

Makes 40 creams.

Chocolate Toffee Pecans

375g (12 oz/1½ cups) sugar
125 ml (4 fl oz/½ cup) water
30 pecan or walnut halves
60g (2 oz) plain (dark) chocolate, chopped

Grease a baking sheet. In a small saucepan, cook sugar and water over low heat until sugar dissolves. Shake pan; do not stir. Remove sugar crystals from sides of pan with a pastry brush dipped in warm water. Adjust heat to medium; cook until a light golden brown. Transfer pan immediately to a frying pan with a small amount of water. Warm over a low heat, so that toffee does not set too quickly.

Drop 6 nuts in pan. Swirl pan gently to coat. Remove each one with a small teaspoon. Do not stir or shake toffee. Place nuts on prepared baking sheet. Let set. Repeat with remaining nuts.

Melt chocolate in a bowl or top of a double boiler set over a pan of simmering water. Stir until smooth. Scoop a little chocolate in a spoon. Dip one end of each toffee-coated nut. Let set on greaseproof paper. Refrigerate in an airtight container with greaseproof paper between layers up to 5 weeks.

Makes 30 pieces.

— Chocolate-Coated Macadamias —

**18 whole macadamia nuts, whole almonds or
   walnut halves
60g (2 oz) plain (dark) chocolate, chopped
60g (2 oz) white chocolate, chopped**

Insert a cocktail stick in each nut. Melt
plain and white chocolate separately in 2
bowls or tops of 2 double boilers set over
pans of simmering water. Stir until smooth.

Scoop plain (dark) chocolate in one spoon,
white chocolate in another. Dip nuts, top ½
in plain chocolate.

Dip bottom ½ in white chocolate. Stick
cocktail sticks into an orange or grapefruit to
set evenly. Refrigerate in a covered
container up to 1 week.

Makes 18 pieces.

Chocolate Almond Toffee

375g (12 oz/1½ cups) sugar
250 ml (8 fl oz/½ cup) water
few drops vanilla essence
60g (2 oz/½ cup) slivered almonds
60g (2 oz) plain (dark) chocolate, chopped

Lightly grease a 27 x 18cm (11 x 7in) pan. Combine sugar and water in a saucepan over low heat. Swirl pan to dissolve sugar. When sugar is dissolved, boil until mixture is a pale golden colour. Remove from heat and add vanilla. Swirl pan to combine and pour toffee into prepared pan.

Place almonds on a baking sheet and toast 10 minutes at 180C (350F/Gas 4), stir occasionally, until almonds are a golden colour. Cool. Melt chocolate in bowl or top of a double boiler set over a pan of simmering water. Stir until smooth. When toffee is firmly set, spread chocolate evenly over toffee using back of a spoon or a small knife.

Sprinkle with almonds and press almonds into chocolate. Let set until firm. Run a sharp knife around the edges. Invert on greaseproof paper and break toffee into small pieces. Store in an airtight container in the refrigerator up to 1 month.

Makes about 50 pieces.

Chocolate Hazelnut Buttons

FILLING: 60g (2 oz/½ cup) hazelnuts
60g (2 oz) plain (dark) chocolate, chopped
60g (2 oz/¼ cup) unsalted butter, diced
1 tablespoon brandy
90g (3 oz) white chocolate, chopped

BUTTONS:

TO DECORATE: slices of hazelnut
grated white chocolate

Place hazelnuts on a baking sheet and toast at 180C (350F/Gas 4) until skins are slightly blistered. Wrap hazelnuts in a towel for 3 minutes. Remove skins by rubbing with towel. Chop nuts finely. To make filling, place plain chocolate, butter and brandy in a bowl or top of a double boiler set over a pan of simmering water. Stir until smooth. Remove from heat, stir in nuts and cool. Refrigerate filling 1 hour or until firm enough to handle.

Melt white chocolate in a bowl or top of a double boiler set over a pan of simmering water and stir until smooth. Form buttons by dropping 1 teaspoon of white chocolate onto greaseproof paper. Smooth out each button to form a flat round.

Form ½ teaspoon of filling into a tiny ball and flatten ball so it is same size as white chocolate button. While white chocolate is still soft, top button with hazelnut filling. Lightly press together. Decorate each button with a slice of hazelnut or grated white chocolate. Refrigerate for 2 hours or until set. To store, layer in a jar leaving each one attached to small piece of greaseproof paper up to 3 weeks.

Makes 24 buttons.

Chocolate Drambuie Strips

60 ml (2 fl oz/¼ cup) thick cream
155g (5 oz) milk chocolate, chopped
2 tablespoons Drambuie

TO FINISH: icing sugar, sifted

Line bottom of baking sheet with greaseproof paper. Heat cream in a small saucepan until bubbling around edges. Remove from heat and add chocolate. Let stand, covered, until chocolate melts. Add Drambuie and mix well. Refrigerate until firm enough to hold soft peaks.

Using a fluted nozzle in a pastry bag, pipe strips onto greaseproof paper. Place immediately in freezer to set.

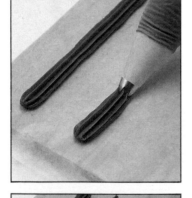

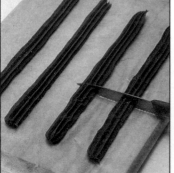

Cut chocolate into strips. Store in freezer with paper between layers for up to 3 months. Remove from the freezer just before serving, as they become creamy within 20 minutes at room temperature. Dust with icing sugar.

Makes 40 pieces.

Coffee Creams

CASES: 125g (4 oz) white chocolate, chopped

COFFEE CREAM FILLING: 4 tablespoons thick cream
60g (2 oz) white chocolate, chopped
2 teaspoons coffee liqueur
2 teaspoons instant coffee powder dissolved in
   1 teaspoon water

TO DECORATE: 24 slices brazil nuts

Line bottom of baking sheet with greaseproof paper. To make cases, melt chocolate in a bowl or top of a double boiler set over a pan of simmering water. Brush a thin layer of chocolate on bottom and sides of small foil cases. Turn cases upside down on baking sheet. Refrigerate to set. Remove and brush a second layer of chocolate on top of first layer. Turn cases upside down on baking sheet. Refrigerate to set.

To make filling, heat cream in a small saucepan until boiling. Add chocolate, and remove from heat. Let stand, covered, until chocolate melts. Mix in coffee liqueur and coffee; stir until smooth.

Fill cases with filling. Decorate with a slice of brazil nut. Chill until set. Peel off foil cases before serving. To store, refrigerate in a covered container up to 1 week.

Makes 24 creams.

Mocha Creams

185g (6 oz) plain (dark) chocolate, chopped
60g (2 oz/¼ cup) butter
1 tablespoon instant coffee powder
1 egg yolk
2 teaspoons rum
60g (2 oz) white chocolate, chopped

Line bottom of baking sheet with greaseproof paper. Melt plain chocolate in bowl or top of a double boiler set over a pan of simmering water; cool. In a medium bowl, cream butter until soft; add instant coffee. Stir in cooled chocolate, egg yolk, and rum. Chill slightly until mixture is of piping consistency.

Using a fluted nozzle in a pastry bag, pipe small rounds with peaks on top on baking sheet. Chill until set.

Melt white chocolate in a bowl or top of a double boiler set over a pan of simmering water. Hold mocha creams by base. Dip peaked tops into white chocolate to coat. Place on baking sheet. Refrigerate to chill. When set, store in a covered container in refrigerator up to 2 weeks.

Makes 40 creams.

Chocolate Cases

125g (4 oz) plain dark or milk chocolate, chopped
24 foil petits four cases

Place a sheet of greaseproof paper on a baking sheet. Melt chocolate in bowl or top of a double boiler set over a pan of simmering water. Stir until smooth; cool slightly. Spoon 1 teaspoon melted chocolate into each foil case. Spread chocolate over bottom and up sides of cases with back of spoon covering insides completely. Place upside-down on prepared baking sheet. Refrigerate 20 minutes or until chocolate is completely set.

Using a pastry brush, recoat insides of cases with remaining melted chocolate. Place on baking sheet. Refrigerate until set.

Refrigerate cases in a sealed container. To serve, fill cases, see pages 26, 27, 28, and peel off foil.

Makes 24 cases.

— Lemon-Filled Chocolate Cases —

18 chocolate cases, see page 25

1 teaspoon powdered gelatine
1 tablespoon cold water
3 tablespoons yogurt
¼ teaspoon grated lemon peel
1 teaspoon lemon juice
1 teaspoon brandy
2 tablespoons icing sugar
1 tablespoon thick cream

TO DECORATE: 30g (1 oz) plain (dark) or
milk chocolate, chopped

Dissolve gelatine in water in a small mixing
bowl or jug placed in pan of hot water.

Mix yogurt with lemon peel, lemon juice,
brandy, sugar and cream. Add yogurt
mixture by spoonfuls to gelatine and blend.

Fill chocolate cases quickly before gelatine
sets. Refrigerate filled cases until set. To
decorate, melt chocolate in small saucepan
over low heat. Spoon chocolate into a pastry
bag fitted with a small plain writing tip. Pipe
chocolate in a small spiral on top of filling.
Refrigerate until set. Store up to 2 days. To
serve, peel off foil.

Makes 18 cases.

Cherry Liqueur-Filled Cases

12 chocolate cases, see page 25

FILLING: 12 sour cherries, stoned
2 tablespoons kirsch, brandy or cognac
1 tablespoon cream
1 teaspoon liquid glucose
30g (1 oz) white chocolate, chopped

Combine cherries and kirsch, brandy or cognac in a small bowl. Cover and refrigerate for 3 days. Stir occasionally. Drain cherries; reserve the kirsch. Place a cherry in a foil-covered chocolate case.

In a small saucepan, cook cream and glucose until cream is bubbling. Add chocolate; remove from heat. Cover and let stand until chocolate melts. Stir until smooth. Add reserved kirsch from cherries.

Cover cherry in chocolate case with chocolate mixture. Refrigerate up to 10 days. To serve peel off foil.

Makes 12 cases.

Fruit-Filled Chocolate Cases

12 chocolate cases, see page 25

FILLING: **45g (1½ oz/¼ cup) mixed glacé fruit, made up of equal parts glacé cherries, apricots, pineapple and ginger, finely chopped**
1 tablespoon brandy
1 rounded tablespoon lightly-whipped cream

TO DECORATE: **12 thin slices glacé cherry**

Combine fruit and brandy in a small bowl. Cover and refrigerate for 24 hours.

Fold cream through fruit mixture. Fill chocolate cases and smooth top.

Decorate with a thin slice of cherry. Refrigerate until firm or up to 2 days. To serve, peel off foil.

Makes 12 cases.

Praline

60g (2 oz/¹⁄₃ cup) almond slivers or hazelnuts
90g (3 oz/¹⁄₂ cup) sugar
60 ml (2 fl oz/¹⁄₄ cup) water

Place nuts on a baking sheet and toast at 180C (350F/Gas 4) for 10 minutes or until golden brown. Stir occasionally to colour evenly. If using hazelnuts, chop finely. Lightly oil another baking sheet. In a medium saucepan, heat sugar and water over low heat until sugar dissolves, shaking pan occasionally. Increase heat and cook until golden. Stir in nuts.

Cook 2–3 minutes, stirring well.

Pour onto prepared sheet; cool. When brittle, finely crush with a meat mallet or process in a blender or processor. Store in an airtight container in refrigerator 3 weeks. Use in truffles, pages 30 and 31, and Praline and Orange Puffs, page 105.

Makes 125g (4 oz/³⁄₄ cup) crushed praline.

Almond Praline Truffles

90g (3 oz/⅓ cup) butter, cubed
125 ml (4 fl oz/½ cup) whipping cream
315g (10 oz) milk chocolate, chopped
2 egg yolks
125g (4 oz/¾ cup) crushed almond praline, see page 29
cocoa, sifted

In a small saucepan, combine butter with cream. Cook on low heat until butter melts and cream bubbles around edges.

Remove from heat; add chocolate. Cover and let stand until chocolate melts. Stir until smooth. Add egg yolks, one at a time. Stir over a low heat until glossy. Mixture should be tepid. Remove from heat; cool. Fold in crushed praline. Refrigerate until firm.

Form into 60 balls. Roll in cocoa and coat completely. Chill until firm. Refrigerate in an airtight container up to 10 days. To serve, place in small paper or foil cases.

Makes 60 truffles.

Hazelnut Praline Truffles

60g (2 oz/¼ cup) butter, cubed
250g (8 oz) plain (dark) chocolate, chopped
125g (4 fl oz/½ cup) thick cream
1 tablespoon dark rum
125g (4 oz/¾ cup) hazelnut praline, see page 29

TO COAT: 45g (1½ oz) plain (dark) chocolate, chopped
45g (1½ oz) milk chocolate, chopped

Melt butter in a small saucepan. Remove from heat and add chocolate. Cover and let stand 3 minutes. Stir until smooth. Add cream a few spoonfuls at a time, stirring well until chocolate is smooth.

Cool mixture. Add rum. Mix in crushed hazelnut praline and stir well. Refrigerate until firm. Form into 60 small balls. Refrigerate to firm.

To coat the truffles, melt plain chocolate in a bowl or top of a double boiler set over a pan of simmering water. Stir until smooth. Repeat procedure for milk chocolate. Dip tops of 30 truffles into plain chocolate. Dip the tops of remaining 30 into milk chocolate. Place on greaseproof paper, chocolate side uppermost. Let set at room temperature. Refrigerate in a covered container with waxed paper between layers up to 10 days.

Makes about 60 truffles.

White Truffles

30g (1 oz/¼ cup) slivered almonds
2 tablespoons finely chopped mixed glacé fruit
3 tablespoons cream
100g (3½ oz) white chocolate, chopped
1 tablespoon kirsch or brandy

TO COAT: 45g (1½ oz/½ cup) dessicated coconut

Toast almonds in a dry frying pan until golden, stirring occasionally. Chop finely. In a small bowl mix almonds with glacé fruits.

Bring cream to a boil in a small saucepan. Add chocolate to cream. Cover and let stand until chocolate softens. Stir until smooth. Mix in kirsch or brandy, nuts and fruit. Refrigerate in a bowl until firm.

Toast coconut in a dry frying pan. Stir until golden; cool. Form truffle mixture into 24 balls. Roll balls in coconut. Store in refrigerator up to 10 days. To serve, place in small paper or foil cases.

Makes 24 truffles.

Orange Truffles

60g (2 oz/¼ cup) butter, chopped
75 ml (2½ fl oz/⅓ cup) thick cream
220g (7 oz) plain (dark) chocolate, chopped
1 egg yolk
1 teaspoon grated orange peel
2 tablespoons finely chopped mixed citrus peel
2 tablespoons Grand Marnier
cocoa, sifted

In a small saucepan, combine butter with cream. Cook on low heat until butter melts and cream bubbles around edge. Remove from heat; add chocolate. Cover and let stand until chocolate melts. Stir until smooth.

Stir in egg yolk. Mix in orange peel, citrus peel, and Grand Marnier. Chill until firm.

Form into 40 balls. Roll in cocoa. Refrigerate in an airtight container up to 2 weeks. To serve, place in small paper or foil cases.

Makes 40 truffles.

Two-Toned Truffles

WHITE CENTRE: 2 teaspoons liquid glucose
60 ml (2 fl oz/¼ cup) thick cream
155g (5 oz) white chocolate, chopped

CHOCOLATE COATING: 60g (2 oz/¼ cup) butter, chopped
200g (6½ oz) plain (dark) chocolate, chopped
3 tablespoons thick cream
2 tablespoons Grand Marnier
cocoa, sifted

To make white centre, combine glucose and cream in a small saucepan. Bring to a boil. Remove from heat and add white chocolate. Leave stand few minutes until white chocolate melts and, if necessary, return to low heat. Pour mixture into a medium bowl lined with foil. Chill until firm. Form mixture into 6 balls. Freeze until firm.

To make chocolate coating, melt butter in a small saucepan on low heat. Add plain chocolate; remove from heat. Stir until smooth. Add cream and Grand Marnier. Chill until slightly firm. To assemble truffles, divide plain chocolate mixture into 6 balls. Flatten each ball. Wrap around white chocolate ball. Roll between hands to form an even surface.

Roll balls in cocoa. Freeze until firm. Wrap each ball in plastic wrap and then in foil. Store in freezer up to 8 weeks. To serve, cut each frozen ball in ½, using a knife dipped in boiling water. Divide each ½ into 3 wedges. Place in small paper cases, white side up.

Makes 36 truffles.

Ginger Truffles

60g (2 oz/¼ cup) butter, cubed
75 ml (2½ fl oz/⅓ cup) cream
½ teaspoon fresh ginger
200g (6½ oz) milk chocolate, chopped
45g (1½ oz/¼ cup) finely chopped glacé ginger
1 egg yolk
1 tablespoon Drambuie
cocoa, sifted

Grate fresh ginger. In a small saucepan, combine butter with cream and fresh ginger. Cook on low heat until butter melts and cream bubbles around edge.

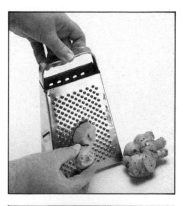

Remove from heat. Add chocolate. Cover and let stand until chocolate melts. Stir until smooth. Mix in glacé ginger and egg yolk. Add Drambuie. Chill 8 hours or until firm.

Form into 40 small balls. Roll in cocoa. Refrigerate up to 3 weeks. To serve, place in small paper or foil cases.

Makes 40 truffles.

Cake Truffles

90g (3 oz/1¼ cup) sponge or butter cake crumbs
grated peel ½ orange
grated peel ½ lemon
2 teaspoons icing sugar
2 teaspoons apricot jam, sieved smooth
2 tablespoons finely chopped glacé cherries
½ teaspoon lemon juice
cocoa, sifted

Place cake crumbs in a medium bowl. Add orange and lemon peel, sugar, jam, cherries and lemon juice. Mix well. If not moist enough to stick together, add a little extra lemon juice.

Form into 20 small balls. Sift cocoa on to greaseproof paper.

Roll balls in cocoa until lightly coated. Shake gently to rid excess cocoa. Refrigerate in a covered container up to 5 days. To serve place in small paper or foil cases.

Makes 20 truffles.

Almond & Prune Truffles

8 prunes, stoned, chopped
2 tablespoons cognac
2 tablespoons blanched almonds, finely chopped
125 ml (4 fl oz/½ cup) thick cream
185g (6 oz) plain (dark) chocolate, chopped
30g (1 oz) butter, melted
cocoa, sifted

Cover prunes with cognac in a small bowl. Let stand 2 hours. Toast almonds in a dry frying ˙pan until light brown. Stir occasionally.

Heat cream in a small saucepan until bubbling around edge. Add chocolate. Remove from heat. Cover and let stand 5 minutes. Stir until smooth. Stir in butter. Drain liquid from prunes. Stir liquid into chocolate mixture. Stir in almonds and prune pieces. Chill until slightly firm.

Form into 40 balls. Roll in cocoa. Refrigerate with greaseproof paper between layers up to 2 weeks. To serve, place in small paper or foil cases.

Makes 40 truffles.

Rum Balls

RUM BALLS: 45g (1½ oz/¾ cup) génoise crumbs,
see page 55
45g (1½ oz/¼ cup) icing sugar
45g (1½ oz/¼ cup) ground almonds
2 teaspoons dark rum
1 teaspoon lemon juice
45g (1½ oz) plain (dark) chocolate, chopped
2 tablespoons cream

ICING: 60g (2 oz/⅓ cup) icing sugar
30g (1 oz) butter, chopped
30g (1 oz) plain (dark) chocolate, grated
2 teaspoons dark rum
warm water

TO DECORATE: chocolate sprinkles

In a medium bowl, combine cake crumbs, sugar, almonds, rum and lemon juice. Melt chocolate in a bowl or top of a double boiler set over a pan of simmering water. Add to rum mixture with sufficient cream for mixture to hold together when pressed between fingers. Form teaspoonfuls of mixture into 18 small balls. Refrigerate on a baking sheet 4 hours or until firm.

To make icing, combine sugar, butter, chocolate and rum in a small saucepan. When chocolate and butter softens, add a tablespoon of water. Warm again and add sufficient water to liquify.

To coat rum balls, insert a skewer in centre of a rum ball. Tilt pan of icing and dip each ball. Let excess drip. To decorate, roll in chocolate sprinkles to coat completely. Refrigerate in a covered container with greaseproof paper between layers up to 10 days.

Makes 18 rum balls.

Christmas Truffles

90g (3 oz/¾ cup) plain sweet biscuits, crushed
2 tablespoons finely chopped glacé cherries
2 tablespoons finely chopped hazelnuts
2 tablespoons ground almonds
2 tablespoons finely chopped mixed citrus peel
2 tablespoons chopped raisins or sultanas
1 tablespoon brandy or rum
few drops almond essence
60g (2 oz/¼ cup) butter, cubed
185g (6 oz) plain (dark) chocolate, chopped
2 tablespoons thick cream

TO COAT: 90g (3 oz/¾ cup) finely chopped
    hazelnuts

In a medium bowl, mix biscuits, cherries,
hazelnuts, almonds, peel, raisins, brandy or
rum and almond essence.

Melt butter in a small saucepan until
bubbling. Add chocolate; remove from heat.
Cover and let stand. Stir occasionally, until
chocolate melts. Add cream; stir into biscuit
mixture. Refrigerate until firm.

Form into 40 small balls. To coat, roll balls
in nuts. Refrigerate in a covered container
with greaseproof paper between layers up to
2 weeks. To serve, place in small paper or foil
cases.

Makes 40 truffles.

Marzipan

250g (8 oz/2 cups) ground almonds
250g (8 oz/1½ cups) icing sugar, sifted
2 teaspoons lemon juice
2 teaspoons sherry or brandy
few drops almond essence, if desired
2 small egg whites
icing sugar

Combine almonds and sugar in medium bowl. Add lemon juice, sherry or brandy, and almond essence if desired.

Gradually mix in enough egg white to ensure that paste is sticky, but not wet.

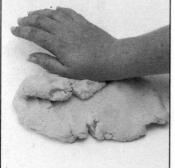

Knead paste until smooth on a pastry board dusted with icing sugar. Wrap in plastic wrap. Store in refrigerator up to 4 weeks. To use, see pages 41, 42, 43, 44, 47, 49, 56, 118.

Makes 500g (1 lb).

Marzipan Cherry Delights

100g (3½ oz) marzipan, see page 40
pink food colouring
1 teaspoon kirsch
90g (3 oz) plain (dark) chocolate, chopped
6 peeled pistachio nuts

Line a plate with greaseproof paper. Knead marzipan with food colouring to shade of pale pink. Add sufficient kirsch so marzipan is slightly sticky but able to hold a shape. Form into 18 small balls. Place on greaseproof paper and refrigerate until firm.

Melt chocolate in a bowl or top of a double boiler set over a pan of simmering water. Stir until smooth. Insert a cocktail stick in top of each marzipan ball. Dip ½ of ball into chocolate. Place balls on greaseproof paper and refrigerate until dry and firm.

Cut pistachio nuts in 3 pieces lengthwise. Remove cocktail sticks and insert pistachio nuts in cavity left by cocktail stick. Store in a covered container in refrigerator up to 10 days.

Makes 18 balls.

Chocolate Marzipan Delights

30g (1 oz) plain (dark) chocolate, chopped
125g (4 oz) homemade marzipan, see page 40
1 egg white
peppermint essence
90g (3 oz) white chocolate, chopped
24 angelica strips

Grate or chop plain chocolate.

Melt plain chocolate in a bowl or top of a double boiler set over a pan of simmering water. Gradually add chocolate to marzipan and knead well. If marzipan becomes dry, add 1 to 2 teaspoons of egg white. Flavour with a few drops of peppermint essence. Form into 24 small balls. Chill for 1 hour to firm.

Melt white chocolate in a bowl or top of a double boiler set over a pan of simmering water. Insert a cocktail stick in top of each marzipan ball and dip base of ball in chocolate. Place on greaseproof paper to set. Remove cocktail stick and insert a strip of angelica in cavity left by cocktail stick. Store in refrigerator in one layer so balls retain stalks. These will keep for about 10 days.

Makes 24 balls.

Marzipan Cherry Log

125g (4 oz) marzipan, see page 40
2 tablespoons icing sugar
30g (1 oz/⅓ cup) dessicated coconut
1 egg white
30g (1 oz/¼ cup) pistachio nuts, shelled
green food colouring
6-8 glacé cherries

TO DECORATE: 45g (1½ oz/½ cup) dessicated coconut

Mix marzipan, sugar, 30g (1 oz/⅓ cup) coconut and egg white in a medium mixing bowl. Mixture should be moist, but not sticky. Knead well; divide into 2 sections. Wrap each section in plastic wrap; chill for 2 hours. Place nuts in a small bowl. Cover with boiling water. Let stand until water is tepid to remove brown skins. Peel and finely chop nuts. Mix nuts and 2 drops green food colouring with 1 marzipan section.

On an icing sugared surface or between 2 sheets of plastic wrap, roll thinly to 20 x 10cm (8 x 4in). Roll second section in same way; trim edges and sides evenly. Top green section with plain section. Cut cherries in ½ and place flat side down in centre of rectangle. Roll 2 sections to enclose cherries.

Toast 45g (1½ oz/½ cup) coconut in a dry frying pan, stirring until light golden brown. Roll log in coconut to completely coat outside. If marzipan is dry, use a pastry brush to moisten with a little water, so coconut will stick. Refrigerate log wrapped in foil. Slice just before serving.

Makes 30 slices.

— Marzipan Fruits & Vegetables —

marzipan, see page 40
caster sugar
food colouring

Mould fruits or vegetables. Dry for 1 day. Paint with food colouring. Cover and refrigerate up to 10 days.

Apple: Form a small ball. Curve sides gently. Make base slightly pointed. Press indentations into sides and top where stalk is attached. Paint red with tinges of green and brown. Place a small clove or a small piece of a strawberry or cherry stalk on top.

Banana: Form a long piece of marzipan, thinner at ends than at centre. Bend slightly to curve. Paint yellow with streaks of brown or green. Use a piece of cherry stalk or clove to make end.

Lemon: Form a ball. Make rounded points at both ends. Gently pinch one point to make an indentation. Paint yellow and tint points light green. Roll on a nutmeg grater to make indents.

Mushroom: Form 2 balls of marzipan. Flatten in 2 rounds. One round should be slightly larger. Place smaller round on top of larger round; fold over edge. Lightly cut inside to resemble markings of a mushroom cap. Form piece of marzipan into a stalk. Place stalk in centre of lower round. Paint outside pale cream to light brown and inside dark brown.

Pear: Form a small ball. Stretch one end slightly to form pear shape. Paint pale green or yellow. Paint diluted red on rounded section to give a ripe appearance. Place on small piece of a strawberry or cherry stalk on tapered end.

—— Marzipan Fruits Continued ——

Strawberry: Form a small ball of marzipan. Pinch slightly to make base longer. Point should be slightly rounded and top flattened. Paint with red colouring. While colouring is wet, drop strawberry into caster sugar. Add a small green leaf of moulded or cut green marzipan.

Watermelon Slices: Form a ball. Flatten into a circle. Cut in half. Let dry. Paint outside dark green. Leave a strip of natural coloured marzipan inside. Paint flat sides and straight edges pink. When dry, paint dark brown seeds.

Orange: Make a small ball. Roll over a grater to make imprints. When dry, paint orange. Attach a tiny piece of stalk, if desired.

Chocolate Marzipan Log

125g (4 oz) marzipan, crumbled, see page 40
45g (1½ oz/¼ cup) icing sugar
1 egg white
75g (2¼ oz/¾ cup) dessicated coconut
angelica strips or glacé apricots, halved
45g (1½ oz) plain (dark) chocolate, chopped

In a medium bowl, mix marzipan and sugar.
Knead small amounts of egg white into
marzipan mixture. Add additional egg white
until a sticky paste forms. Add coconut and
knead for 1 minute. If too sticky, knead on a
icing sugar surface. Chill mixture 30
minutes.

Form a long roll 30 x 15cm (12 x 6in) on
plastic wrap. Place angelica strips or glacé
apricots along one side. Roll marzipan over
to enclose fruit. Wrap well; chill 12 hours.

Melt chocolate in a bowl or top of a double
boiler set over a pan of simmering water. Stir
until smooth. Unwrap almond roll and
spread one side with chocolate. When set,
turn log over and spread chocolate on other
side. When set, wrap and chill. Refrigerate
whole up to 3 weeks. To serve, cut into slices
as needed.

Makes 24 slices.

Glazed Apricot Pecans

40 pecan or walnut halves

APRICOT PURÉE: 60g (2 oz/½ cup) dried apricots
2 tablespoons icing sugar
30g (1 oz/¼ cup) ground almonds
1 teaspoon brandy

TOFFEE: 250g (8 oz/1 cup) sugar
75 ml (2½ fl oz/⅓ cup) water

In a small saucepan, cook apricots covered with water until soft. Drain; purée apricots.

In a medium bowl, combine apricots, icing sugar, almonds and brandy. Chill 2 hours before using. Refrigerate up to 2 days. Place a teaspoon of apricot mixture on a nut; top with another nut. Press together gently. Remove excess apricot mixture.

Grease a wire rack and baking sheet. Place wire rack over baking sheet. In a small saucepan, cook sugar and water over low heat. Swirl mixture occasionally until sugar dissolves. Adjust heat to medium. Cook until mixture is a light golden brown. Remove from heat. Quickly drop nuts, one-by-one, into toffee. Using a small spoon, remove immediately; cool on wire rack. Refrigerate in a covered container up to 12 hours.

Makes 20 pieces

French Prunes

16 prunes
60g (2 oz) marzipan, see page 40
green food colouring

TOFFEE COATING: 250g (8 oz/1 cup) sugar
75 ml (2½ fl oz/⅓ cup) water

In a small bowl, cover prunes with boiling water. Let stand 15 minutes. Drain and spread on paper towels. Cut a slit in one side of each prune; remove stone.

Knead marzipan, add 1 to 2 drops green food colouring. Form marzipan into 16 balls. Roll balls to an oval. Insert shaped marzipan into prune cavity left by stone. Mould prune to leave green section showing. Let dry for 3 hours.

To make toffee, warm sugar and water in a small saucepan over low heat until sugar has dissolved. Adjust heat to medium; cook until mixture turns light golden brown. Shake pan occasionally. Brush sugar crystals on side of pan away with a pastry brush dipped in cold water. Remove from heat. Pierce each prune through side with a cocktail stick. Place prunes on a wire rack set over a baking tray. Tilt saucepan of toffee. Quickly dip each prune holding by cocktail stick or dipping tool to coat with toffee. Let stand on wire rack until set. Refrigerate in a single layer up to 12 hours.

Makes 16 prunes.

Caramel-Glazed Fruit

12 medium-sized strawberries
or 12 mandarin segments
or 18 cherries
or 10 bunches of grapes, 2 grapes to 1 bunch

CARAMEL: 375g (12 oz/1½ cups) sugar
75 ml (2½ fl oz/⅓ cup) water
pinch of cream of tartar

If using grapes or cherries, wash and let drain 2 hours on paper towels. If using strawberries, clean with a pastry brush. Leave stalks on fruit. If using mandarins, peel fruit and separate segments. Remove membrane. Dry mandarin segments on a wire rack 3-4 hours. Push a cocktail stick into mandarin segments.

Lightly grease a baking sheet. To make caramel, in a small saucepan, warm sugar and water over low heat until sugar has dissolved. Shake pan occasionally. When sugar has dissolved, add cream of tartar. Adjust heat to high; cook until caramel becomes light gold. Brush away sugar crystals on side of pan away with a pastry brush dipped in cold water. Do not stir syrup.

Immediately dip fruits. Let excess caramel drip over saucepan. Place on prepared baking sheet. Let stand until set. Place in paper cases and serve within 4 hours.

Makes 10-18 pieces.

Apricot & Ginger Balls

30g (1 oz) hazelnuts
10 dried apricot halves
1 tablespoon finely chopped glacé ginger
2 teaspoons icing sugar

TO COVER 50g (1¾ oz/½ cup) ground almonds
30g (1 oz/¼ cup) sugar
1 teaspoon lemon juice
egg white

TOPPING: 50g (1¾ oz/½ cup) almonds, finely
chopped

Preheat oven to 180C (350F/Gas 4). Roast
hazelnuts in preheated oven on baking
sheet 10 minutes or until golden brown and
skins have slightly blistered. Wrap in a
towel; let stand 2 minutes. Rub them in the
towel to remove skins. Chop nuts finely. In a
small saucepan, cook apricots covered with
water, until softened. Drain; dry on paper
towels. Chop apricots.

In a small bowl mix hazelnuts, apricots,
ginger and sugar. Refrigerate 1 hour or until
firm. Form mixture into 18 small balls.
Refrigerate on a plate. To make covering, in
a small bowl, mix ground almonds, sugar
and lemon juice. Add ½ to 1 teaspoon egg
white to form a sticky but firm paste. Chill 2
hours.

Form 18 small balls from covering mixture.
Flatten; place an apricot ginger ball in
centre. Fold to partly enclose. Leave top of
apricot ball showing. Dip apricot top in
chopped almonds to coat thickly. Refrigerate
in a covered container with greaseproof
paper between layers up to 10 days.

Makes 18 balls.

Fruit Pyramids

60g (2 oz/⅓ cup) dried figs, chopped
60g (2 oz/⅓ cup) dates, stoned, finely chopped
30g (1 oz) glacé cherries, finely chopped
60g (2 oz/½ cup) dried apricots, finely chopped
60g (2 oz/⅓ cup) pine nuts, finely chopped
2 teaspoons lemon juice
60g (2 oz/⅓ cup) icing sugar

TO COAT: **dessicated coconut**

In a small bowl, mix figs, dates and cherries. Cover apricots with boiling water in a small bowl. Let stand 2 minutes. Drain well; add to other fruit.

Mix pine nuts, lemon juice and sugar with fruit. Mixture should bind together when pressed between fingers. If too firm, moisten with lemon juice.

Toast coconut in a dry frying pan. Stir frequently until a pale golden brown. Form fruit mixture into 36 small balls. Roll in coconut. Pinch tops to form pyramids. Chill 2 hours on a plate. Refrigerate in a covered container in a single layer or with foil between layers up to 3 weeks.

Makes 36 pieces.

Candied Grapefruit Peel

2 large thick skinned grapefruit
375g (12 oz/1½ cups) sugar
250 ml (8 fl oz/1 cup) water
caster sugar

Cut each grapefruit in ½; discard pulp. Cut each ½ of peel in 4 pieces. Cut peel pieces in triangular shapes or strips. Each grapefruit should yield about 40 pieces.

In a small saucepan, bring grapefruit peel, covered with cold water, to a boil over medium heat. Drain. Repeat procedure 6 times, cooking peel the last time until soft. Drain. In a small saucepan, cook sugar and water over low heat until sugar dissolves. Adjust heat to medium, bring to a boil. Add pieces of peel. Cook uncovered until sections are clear and transparent. Using a slotted spoon, remove peel to a wire rack set over a baking sheet. Separate pieces; let set 48 hours or until firm.

In a medium bowl, dust peel with sugar. Dry on a wire rack 6 hours. Refrigerate in a covered container up to 4 weeks.

Makes about 80 pieces.

Honey Nut Fruit Balls

90g (3 oz/³⁄₄ cup) pine nuts
1 tablespoon vegetable oil
60g (2 oz/¹⁄₃ cup) glacé cherries, finely chopped
60g (2 oz/¹⁄₃ cup) stoned dates, finely chopped
60g (2 oz/¹⁄₃ cup) mixed citrus peel, chopped
90g (3 oz/³⁄₄ cup) pecans, finely chopped
¹⁄₂ teaspoon cinnamon
2 tablespoons honey
60g (2 oz/¹⁄₂ cup) ground almonds
1 egg white

In a frying pan, fry pine nuts with oil over medium heat. Stir until nuts are golden brown. Drain on paper towels. Chop medium fine.

In a small bowl, mix all fruits with pecans and cinnamon. In a small saucepan, warm honey over low heat. Add honey to fruits; mix well. Add ground almonds and enough egg white so mixture will hold together when pressed between fingers. Cool 15 minutes.

Form into 50 small balls. Roll balls in pine nuts to lightly coat. Chill on a plate. Refrigerate in an airtight container with greaseproof paper between layers up to 2 weeks. To serve, place in small paper or foil cases.

Makes 50 balls

Plain Génoise

3 eggs
100g (3½ oz/½ cup) caster sugar
few drops vanilla essence
100g (3½ oz/½ cup) plain flour, sifted
30g (1 oz) butter, melted and cooled

Preheat oven to 180C (350F/Gas 4). Grease and flour bottom and sides of a 30 x 30cm (12 x 12in) baking pan. Shake out excess flour.

Combine eggs and sugar in a medium mixing bowl. Place bowl in a pan of hot water. Beat until mixture is very thick and just warm. Mixture should form a ribbon when beaters are lifted. Remove from heat and add vanilla. Continue beating until mixture is almost cool. Fold flour into egg and sugar mixture. Mix in butter.

Pour mixture into prepared greased pan; level top. Bake in a preheated oven 20-25 minutes or until set on top. Cool pan on a wire rack 10 minutes. Run a knife carefully around the edge. Remove from pan. Cool completely on wire rack. Use within 36 hours or wrap and freeze up to 6 weeks. To use, see pages 38, 56, 60, 64.

Makes 1 30 x 30 cm (12 x 12 in) cake.

Iced Petits Fours

⅓ plain génoise, see page 55

TOPPING: 155g (5 oz/½ cup) apricot jam
1 tablespoon water
90g (3 oz) marzipan, see page 40

ICING: 1 tablespoon liquid glucose
3-4 tablespoons warm water
250g (8 oz/2 cups) icing sugar
few drops food colouring, if desired

To make topping, press jam through a fine strainer into a small saucepan; stir in water. Cook, stirring, 1-2 minutes or until mixture is smooth. Cool slightly. Brush over top of cake.

Roll out marzipan thinly between 2 pieces of plastic wrap. Remove 1 sheet of plastic wrap from marzipan. Place cake on top of marzipan. Trim edges the same size as the cake.

Chill 30 minutes. Invert and peel off plastic wrap.

Using a very sharp knife, cut cake into 2.5cm (1in) squares and chill until firm. Place on wire rack set over a baking sheet.

If making round petits fours, use a pastry cutter to cut circles of cake. Brush top and sides with topping. Cut circles of marzipan with pastry cutter. Place on top of cake. To coat sides, roll on strip of marzipan.

To make icing, combine glucose and 2 tablespoons water in a bowl or top of a double boiler set over a pan of simmering water. Add icing sugar and mix well. Add 1 to 2 more tablespoons of warm water. Warm until mixture is smooth. Tint with food colouring, if desired. Carefully spoon icing over marzipanned cake. Leave to set. Decorate with flowers or fruit or pipe with melted chocolate.

Makes 27 petits fours.

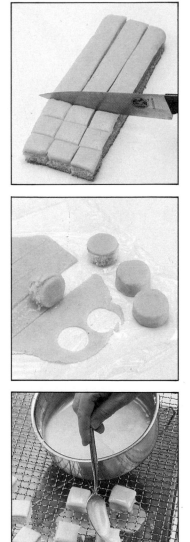

Chocolate Génoise

3 eggs
100g (3½ oz/½ cup) caster sugar
few drops vanilla essence
70g (2¼ oz/½ cup) plain flour
¼ teaspoon ground cinnamon
30g (1 oz/¼ cup) cocoa
30g (1 oz) butter, melted and cooled

Preheat oven to 180C (350F/Gas 4). Grease and flour bottom and sides of a 30 x 30cm (12 x 12in) baking pan. Shake off excess flour. Combine eggs and sugar in a medium mixing bowl. Place bowl in a pan of hot water. Beat until mixture is very thick and just warm. Mixture should form a ribbon when beaters are lifted. Remove from heat and add vanilla. Continue beating until mixture is almost cool. Sift flour, cinnamon and cocoa together. Fold ½ of flour into egg and sugar. Repeat with remaining flour mixture.

Mix in butter. Pour mixture into prepared greased pan; level top. Bake in preheated oven 30-35 minutes or until set on top. Cool pan on a wire rack 10 minutes.

Run knife carefully around edge. Remove from pan. Cool completely on a wire rack. Use within 24 hours or wrap and freeze up to 6 weeks. To use, see page 62.

Makes 1 30 x 30 cm (12 x 12 in) cake.

Petits Fours Siciliana

CAKE: 3 egg yolks
3 tablespoons sugar
2 tablespoons cocoa
few drops vanilla essence
3 egg whites

FILLING: 90g (3 oz/¾ cup) ricotta or cottage cheese
3 tablespoons icing sugar
2 tablespoons orange liqueur
1½ tablespoons finely-chopped mixed citrus peel
3 tablespoons grated plain (dark) chocolate
TO COAT: cocoa

Preheat oven to 180C (350F/Gas 4). Grease bottom and sides 30 x 20cm (12 x 8in) baking pan. Line the bottom with greaseproof paper. Grease and lightly flour paper. Shake off excess flour. In a medium bowl, beat egg yolks with sugar until light. Sift in cocoa; add vanilla. In a small bowl, beat egg whites until stiff. Gently fold into egg yolks, ½ at a time.

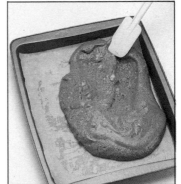

Spread mixture evenly in prepared pan. Bake in preheated oven 10 to 12 minutes or until set. Cool in pan on wire rack 10 minutes. Invert cake on greaseproof paper; peel greaseproof paper off bottom of cake. To store cake, wrap in plastic wrap up to 24 hours.

To make filling, in a small bowl, beat or process cheese until smooth. Add sugar, orange liqueur, peel and chocolate. Mix well. Trim edges from cake. Cut in ½; place on a flat surface. Spread bottom with filling; press other ½ gently on top. Cut cake in 20 slices. Sift cocoa over top. Refrigerate 2 hours. To store, refrigerate in a covered container up to 2 days.

Makes 20 slices.

Grand Marnier Petits Fours

⅓ plain génoise, see page 55

GRAND MARNIER CREAM: 60g (2 oz) unsalted butter
3 tablespoons icing sugar
½ teaspoon grated orange peel
1 egg yolk
1 tablespoon Grand Marnier

ICING: 1 tablespoon liquid glucose
3 tablespoons water
1 tablespoon Grand Marnier
250g (8 oz/2 cups) icing sugar
yellow food colouring

TO DECORATE: angelica strips

Trim edges of cake and cut into two 25cm (10in) long strips. To make Grand Marnier cream, combine butter, icing sugar and orange peel in a medium bowl and beat until soft and smooth. Add egg yolk and Grand Marnier in small amounts until thoroughly blended. If mixture separates, place in a bowl set in warm water, and whisk with a fork until smooth. Chill until cream will hold a shape.

Spread top of cake with Grand Marnier cream. Place remaining cream in a piping bag with a star tube and decorate cake. Chill cake until cream is hard. Cut each strip of cake into 10 pieces. Place cake on a wire rack set over a baking sheet.

To make icing, cook glucose and water in a medium saucepan until glucose has melted and water is just bubbling. Stir in Grand Marnier and icing sugar. Remove from heat and beat until smooth. Reheat until tepid. If icing is too thick, add 1 teaspoon of water. Tint icing with yellow food colouring. Spoon icing over cakes. Let stand until icing is set. Decorate with angelica strips.
Makes 20 petits fours.

Nut Cakes with Lemon Syrup

30g (1 oz/¼ cup) ground walnuts
30g (1 oz/¼ cup) ground almonds
1 tablespoon finely-crushed sweet biscuits
grated peel of ½ lemon
1 egg yolk
2 tablespoons caster sugar
1 egg white
LEMON SYRUP: 60g (2 oz/¼ cup) sugar
1 tablespoon lemon juice
60 ml (2 fl oz/¼ cup) water
1 tablespoon dark or white rum
TOPPING: 90g (3 oz/¼ cup) apricot jam
2 teaspoons lemon juice
TO DECORATE: walnut pieces or almond flakes

Preheat oven to 180C (350F/Gas 4). Grease 12 miniature tart pans. In a small bowl, mix nuts with biscuit crumbs. Add lemon peel. In a small bowl, beat egg yolk with sugar until fluffy. In a small bowl beat egg white until stiff. Fold into egg yolk mixture. Add dry ingredients to eggs, ½ at a time, folding in gently. Fill tart pans ¾ full of mixture. Bake in preheated oven 15 minutes or until firm. Cool 2 minutes before soaking with syrup.

To make syrup, in a small saucepan, bring sugar, lemon juice and water to the boil over medium heat. Simmer 1 minute. Remove from heat. Add rum; cool until tepid. Pour syrup over cakes while still in tart pans. Cool cakes completely. Carefully run a knife around edge to remove cake from tart pan. Place on a wire rack set over a baking sheet.

To make topping, in a small saucepan, heat the jam and lemon juice. Sieve if lumpy. Warm before brushing over top of cakes. Decorate cakes with a walnut piece or almond flake. Let stand 6 hours. Store covered up to 48 hours.
Makes 12 cakes.

Chocolate Boxes

⅓ chocolate génoise, see page 58, cut into 18 squares
220g (7 oz) plain (dark) chocolate, chopped

BUTTER CREAM: 2 teaspoons instant coffee powder
2 teaspoons hot water
90g (3 oz/⅓ cup) butter, room temperature
4 tablespoons icing sugar
1 egg yolk
2 teaspoons brandy or cognac

125g (4 oz/⅓ cup) apricot jam

TO DECORATE: crystallized violet

Line a baking sheet with greaseproof paper. Melt chocolate in a bowl or top of a double boiler set over a pan of simmering water. Stir until smooth. Let cool slightly. Spread melted chocolate onto greaseproof paper to a square 30 x 30cm (12 x 12in). Let set at room temperature.

When set, with a sharp knife, score into 90 squares equivalent to size of cake sides. Cut 18 squares for cake tops. Trim to exact size if necessary. Peel away greaseproof paper.

To make butter cream, dissolve coffee in hot water in a medium mixing bowl. Cream butter with instant coffee and sugar until soft. Add egg yolk. If mixture curdles, place bowl in warm water. Beat until smooth. Add brandy or cognac. Refrigerate to firm slightly.

Sieve jam and warm in a small saucepan until bubbling. Brush cake tops generously with jam.

Place ¼ teaspoon of butter cream on underside of 4 chocolate pieces. Press 1 chocolate piece on each of the cake's 4 sides. Spoon butter cream into a pastry bag fitted with fluted nozzle. Pipe butter cream along one edge of box.

Place a chocolate lid on top, tilting slightly so cream on one side is visible. Decorate with crystallized violet. Repeat procedure for remaining 17 boxes. Chill for several hours until firm. Refrigerate boxes up to 24 hours. Remove 1 hour before serving.

Makes 18 boxes.

Miniature Lamingtons

⅓ plain génoise, see page 55

ICING: 500g (1 lb/3 cups) icing sugar
3 tablespoons cocoa
30g (1 oz) butter, melted
warm water
dessicated coconut

Cut génoise into 24 small rectangles.

In a medium bowl, sift sugar and cocoa into butter. Mix in enough warm water to make an icing.

Drop each cake into icing. Turn over to lightly coat on all sides. Remove; place on a wire rack set over a baking sheet. Spoon coconut on top or carefully roll each piece in a small bowl of coconut. Let set. Store in a covered container with greaseproof paper between layers up to 1 week.

Makes 24 cakes.

Julian's Fruit Cake

500g (1 lb/3 cups) dates, stoned
125g (4 oz/²⁄₃ cup) mixed citrus peel
125g (4 oz/²⁄₃ cup) red glacé cherries
125g (4 oz/²⁄₃ cup) green glacé cherries
125g (4 oz/²⁄₃ cup) sultanas
185g (6 oz/1½ cups) walnuts
100g (3½ oz/1 cup) ground almonds
½ teaspoon baking powder
4 eggs
1 teaspoon cinnamon
½ teaspoon grated nutmeg
2 tablespoons honey
1 to 2 tablespoons whisky

TO GLAZE: apricot jam, if desired

Preheat oven to 180C (350F/Gas 4). Grease
and line a 25 x 25cm (10 x 10in) pan with
greaseproof paper. In a large bowl mix fruits
and walnuts. Add the almonds, baking
powder, eggs, cinnamon, nutmeg, honey
and 1 tablespoon of whisky. Mix well.

Pour into prepared pan. Bake in preheated
oven 1 hour or until top is set.

Cool in pan 10 minutes. Brush with
remaining whisky, if desired. Remove from
pan; cool completely on a wire rack. Wrap in
plastic wrap; let set 48 hours. Cut into 40
small diamonds, squares or strips. To glaze,
brush with apricot jam if desired. Refrigerate
wrapped up to 1 month.

Makes 40 pieces.

Panforte

185g (6 oz/1½ cups) slivered almonds
185g (6 oz/1½ cups) hazelnuts
60g (2 oz/⅓ cup) glacé cherries, coarsely chopped
60g (2 oz/⅓ cup) mixed citrus peel
90g (3 oz/½ cup) glacé apricots, coarsely chopped
90g (3 oz/½ cup) glacé pineapple, coarsely chopped
3 teaspoons cinnamon
2 rounded tablespoons cocoa
90g (3 oz/⅔ cup) flour
155g (5 oz/⅔ cup) sugar
375g (12 oz/1 cup) honey

Preheat oven to 170C (325F/Gas 3). Grease a 30 x 30cm (12 x 12in) baking pan. Line bottom of pan with baking paper. Roast almonds and hazelnuts on separate baking sheets in preheated oven. Stir almonds once or twice until golden brown. Roast hazelnuts until skins blister. Wrap hazelnuts in a towel for 1 minute. Rub towel to loosen skins. Coarsely chop nuts. Mix with cherries, peel, apricots, pineapple, cinnamon, cocoa and flour.

Cook sugar and honey in a small saucepan until mixture reaches soft ball stage 112C (234F). Immediately pour syrup over fruit and nuts; mix well. Pour into greased pan. Dampen hands and press mixture to an even thickness.

Bake in preheated oven 30 minutes or until set on the edges. Test top by touching with back of a spoon. Cool in pan on wire rack 10 minutes. Remove from pan and peel off paper. Cool completely on a wire rack. Store in a covered container 1 week before serving.

Makes about 50 pieces.

Brazil Nut Bread

60g (2 oz/⅓ cup) brazil nuts
3 egg whites
pinch of salt
90g (3 oz/½ cup) caster sugar
90g (3 oz/¾ cup) plain flour
1 teaspoon cinnamon
½ teaspoon nutmeg, freshly ground

Preheat oven to 180C (350F/Gas 4). Grease a 20 x 7.5cm (8 x 3in) loaf pan. Line bottom and sides of pan with greaseproof paper. Roast brazil nuts on a baking sheet until golden. Remove nuts; wrap in a towel. Let stand 5 minutes. Rub towel until skins are removed.

Beat egg whites with salt until stiff. Add ½ sugar; beat again. When stiff, fold in remaining sugar. Sift flour with spices. Gently fold into egg whites. When partly folded, add nuts. Continue folding until no flour is visible. Spoon mixture into loaf pan and smooth top. Bake in preheated oven 25 to 30 minutes or until top is set. Cool in loaf pan on a wire rack for 10 minutes. Remove from pan and cool completely on wire rack. Peel off paper and wrap in foil. Refrigerate 24 hours or freeze up to 4 to 6 weeks before second baking.

Preheat oven to 150C (300F/Gas 2). Using a serrated knife cut the bread into thin slices. If frozen, partly thaw before slicing. Bake slices on a baking sheet in preheated oven 15 minutes or until golden. Turn slices over and bake 10 to 15 minutes or until crisp. Cool slices on baking sheet. Store in an airtight container up to 3 weeks.

Makes 40 slices.

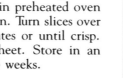

Almond Orange Bread

2 oranges
1 lemon
3 egg whites
pinch of salt
90g (3 oz/½ cup) caster sugar
90g (3 oz/⅔ cup) plain flour
90g (3 oz/½ cup) unblanched whole almonds

Remove peel from 1 orange. Place peel in a small saucepan. Cover with cold water. Bring slowly to a boil; drain and rinse under cold running water. Dry on a paper towel. Grate peel of second orange and lemon. Mix with cooked peel.

Preheat oven to 180C (350F/Gas 4). Grease a 20 x 7.5cm (8 x 3in) loaf pan; line bottom of pan with greaseproof paper. Beat egg whites with salt until stiff. Add sugar and beat again. Mix in orange and lemon peel. Gently fold in flour. When ½ mixture has been folded, add almonds. Continue folding until no flour is visible.

Spoon mixture into loaf pan and smooth top. Bake in preheated oven 35 to 40 minutes or until top is set. Cool in loaf pan on a wire rack 10 minutes. Remove from pan and cool completely on wire rack. Peel off paper and wrap in foil. Refrigerate overnight or freeze up to 4 to 6 weeks before second baking. Preheat oven to 300F (150C). Using a serrated knife, cut bread into thin slices. If frozen partly thaw before slicing. Bake slices on an ungreased baking sheet in preheated oven 15 minutes or until golden. Turn slices over and bake 10 to 15 minutes or until very crisp. Cool slices on baking sheet. Store in an airtight container up to 3 weeks.

Makes 40 slices.

Chocolate Lemon Cheesecakes

CREAM CHEESE FILLING: 125g (4 oz/½ cup) cream
cheese, softened
1 egg
2 tablespoons caster sugar
1 tablespoon lemon juice
CHOCOLATE CAKE: 90g (3 oz/¾ cup) plain flour
125g (4 oz/½ cup) caster sugar
2 tablespoons cocoa
½ teaspoon bicarbonate of soda
½ teaspoon baking powder
pinch of salt
125ml (4 fl oz/½ cup) water
2 tablespoons vegetable oil
2 teaspoons lemon juice
few drops vanilla essence
2 egg yolks
2 egg whites
TO COAT: 60g (2 oz) plain (dark) chocolate
TO DECORATE: crystallized violet, if desired

Preheat oven to 180C (350F/Gas 4). Grease
bottom and sides of 40 miniature tart pans.
Beat cream cheese with egg, sugar and
lemon juice until soft and smooth.

Sift flour with sugar, cocoa, soda, baking
powder and salt. Add water, oil, lemon
juice, vanilla and egg yolks. Beat mixture 30
seconds. In a small bowl, beat egg whites
until stiff. Fold into mixture ⅓ at a time. Fill
tart pans ½ full of chocolate mixture. Drop
a teaspoonful of filling in centre of each.
Bake in preheated oven 12 minutes.

Cool cakes on baking sheet set on wire rack
2 minutes. Carefully run a knife around edge
to remove cake from tart pan. Cool on a
wire rack. Store in a covered container up to
36 hours. Melt chocolate in a bowl or top of
a double boiler set over a pan of simmering
water. Invert cakes on a baking sheet. Cover
bottom with chocolate. Decorate with
crystallized violet.

Makes 40 cheesecakes.

Frosted Almond Biscuits

125g (4 oz/½ cup) butter
grated peel of lemon
100g (3½ oz/½ cup) caster sugar
few drops vanilla essence
125g (4 oz/1 cup) plain flour
50g (1¾ oz/⅓ cup) unblanched almonds, ground
2 egg whites
155g (5 oz/1¼ cups) flaked almonds

TO FINISH: icing sugar

In a medium bowl, cream butter, lemon peel
and sugar until fluffy. Add vanilla and flour.
Mix well to a soft dough, adding almonds.
Chill 1 hour or until firm enough to handle.
Preheat oven to 170C (325F/Gas 3). Grease
a baking sheet.

Roll teaspoonfuls of dough into 50 cylinders.
Flatten to make a log shape. In a small bowl,
whisk egg whites. Dip logs in egg whites,
then in almond flakes. Replace almond
flakes when they become sticky with egg
white.

Place logs close together on prepared baking
sheet. Bake in preheated oven 15 to 20
minutes or until a light golden brown.
Loosen logs from baking sheet. Sift sugar
over top while still warm. Cool on baking
sheet on wire rack. Store in an airtight
container up to 2 weeks.

Makes 50 biscuits.

Sugared Hearts

60g (2 oz/¼ cup) butter
60g (2 oz/⅓ cup) icing sugar
1 egg yolk
few drops vanilla essence
90g (3 oz/⅔ cup) plain flour
1 tablespoon finely chopped blanched almonds

TO FINISH: icing sugar

In a medium bowl, cream butter and sugar until fluffy. Add egg yolk and vanilla; mix in flour. Toast almonds in a dry frying pan until light golden brown, stirring frequently; cool. Mix almonds into sugar mixture and blend thoroughly. Form into a ball. Chill if sticky.

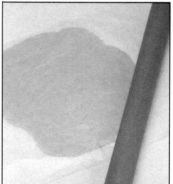

Preheat oven to 180C (350F/Gas 4). Grease a baking sheet. Roll pastry thinly between sheets of greaseproof paper.

Cut dough into 80 hearts with a small, floured heart cutter. Place hearts on prepared baking sheet. Bake in preheated oven 15 to 20 minutes or until a light golden colour. Sift sugar over hearts while still warm. Cool on a wire rack. Store in an airtight container with greaseproof paper between layers up to 10 days.

Makes 80 hearts.

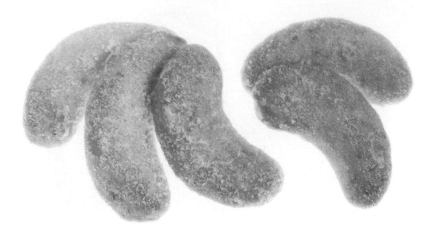

—— Viennese Almond Crescents ——

125g (4 oz/1 cup) plain flour
2 tablespoons sugar
125g (4 oz/½ cup) butter, cubed
60g (2 oz/½ cup) unblanched almonds
1 egg yolk

TO COAT: **caster sugar**

Preheat oven to 180C (350F/Gas 4). Grease a baking sheet. In a medium bowl, sift flour; add sugar. With a pastry blender or 2 knives, cut in butter until mixture resembles coarse crumbs. Chop almonds finely. Add almonds and egg yolk to flour mixture. Knead lightly in bowl until mixture binds well and is sticky. Chill 20 minutes.

Roll 1 teaspoon of pastry into a small log; form a crescent. Repeat. Place crescents close together on prepared baking sheet. Bake in preheated oven 15 minutes or until light golden.

Remove from baking sheet. Spoon sugar over crescents. Cool on a wire rack. Store in an airtight container up to 2 weeks.

Makes 50 crescents.

Iced Biscuit Crisps

60g (2 oz/½ cup) self-raising flour
pinch of salt
1 tablespoon caster sugar
30g (1 oz) butter, cubed
1 egg yolk

ICING: 60g (2 oz/⅓ cup) icing sugar
1 egg white

TO DECORATE: 30g (1 oz/¼ cup) finely-chopped
blanched almonds

Grease 2 baking sheets. In a medium bowl, sift flour with salt; add sugar. With a pastry blender or 2 knives, cut in butter until mixture resembles coarse crumbs. Add egg yolk; mix to a paste. Knead lightly in bowl, form into a ball. Wrap and chill 30 minutes.

Roll pastry between pieces of greaseproof paper or on a lightly floured surface. Cut pastry with a floured 2½cm (1in) round cutter. Place biscuit on prepared baking sheets.

Preheat oven to 180C (350F/Gas 4). To make icing, beat sugar and egg white together. Place 1 teaspoon icing in centre of each biscuit. Smooth slightly. Top biscuits with almonds. Bake in preheated oven 15 to 18 minutes or until a light golden brown. Remove from baking sheet; cool on a wire rack. Store in an airtight container up to 2 weeks.

Makes 50 biscuits.

Glazed Almond Squares

60g (2 oz/¼ cup) butter
125g (4 oz/½ cup) caster sugar
125g (4 oz/1¼ cups) ground almonds
2 eggs
2 tablespoons plain flour

TOPPING: 60g (2 oz/¼ cup) butter
90g (3 oz/⅓ cup) sugar
60 ml (2 fl oz/¼ cup) liquid glucose
90 g (3 oz/¾ cup) almond flakes

Preheat oven to 180C (350F/Gas 4). Grease bottom and sides of a swiss roll tin. In a medium bowl, cream butter and sugar until light and fluffy. Add ground almonds, eggs and flour and mix well. Spread mixture evenly in prepared pan. Bake in preheated oven 10 minutes until golden.

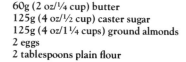

To make topping, melt butter, sugar and glucose in a small saucepan over low heat. Stir in almond flakes. Cook over medium heat 2 minutes. Pour topping over baked biscuit layer; spread evenly.

Bake 5 to 8 minutes until golden brown. Cool in pan on wire rack 10 minutes. Cut into 2½-inch squares. Cool completely in pan on wire rack. Store in an airtight container up to 1 week.

Makes 50 squares.

Chocolate Chip Bars

125g (4 oz/½ cup) butter
90g (3 oz/½ cup) light brown sugar
few drops vanilla essence
pinch of salt
125g (4 oz/1 cup) plain flour
100g (3½ oz) plain (dark) chocolate pieces
60g (2 oz/½ cup) finely chopped walnuts

Preheat oven to 180C (350F/Gas 4). Grease a 27 x 18cm (11 x 7in) baking pan. In a medium bowl cream butter with sugar until fluffy. Add vanilla and mix. Sift salt and flour; add to sugar mixture. Fold in chocolate pieces and walnuts.

Press evenly in prepared pan. Bake in preheated oven 15 to 18 minutes.

Remove from pan ; cool on a wire rack. When cold, cut into 60 bars. Store in airtight container up to 2 weeks.

Makes 60 bars.

Palmiers

185g (6oz) puff pastry
caster sugar

Grease 2 baking sheets. On a sugared surface, roll puff pastry to a long 46 × 30cm (18 × 12in) rectangle. Divide into 2 sections, 23 × 15cm (9 × 6in). Fold one side to the centre and fold second side to meet. Flatten slightly.

Fold both sides to centre. Press down firmly; chill.

With a very sharp knife, cut 40 thin slices. Dip a flexible spatula in sugar. Press on puff pastry slice to flatten. With a rolling pin, roll very thin. Place Palmiers about 1 inch apart on prepared baking sheets. Refrigerate 30 minutes. They may be frozen at this stage and baked later without thawing. Preheat oven to 220C (425F/Gas 7). Bake in preheated oven 5 minutes or until golden. Using a spatula, turn Palmiers over. Bake until golden. Remove from baking sheets; cool on a wire rack. Store in an airtight container up to 2 weeks.

Makes 40 biscuits.

Cigarettes Russes

2 large egg whites
100g (3½ oz/½ cup) caster sugar
90g (3 oz/⅓ cup) butter, melted
few drops vanilla essence
75g (2½ oz/½ cup) plain flour

Preheat oven to 190C (375F/Gas 5). Grease and flour 2 baking sheets. Shake off excess flour. In a medium bowl, beat egg whites with sugar until smooth. Add butter and vanilla. Mix in flour.

Drop a teaspoonful of mixture on prepared baking sheet. Using a knife, spread mixture thinly and evenly to form a circle 10cm (4in) in diameter. Make only 2 or 3 Cigarettes at a time as they need to be rolled quickly while warm and it is difficult to handle more than this. Bake in preheated oven 5-6 minutes or until golden brown.

Using a spatula, remove biscuit from baking sheet. Roll immediately around handle of a wooden spoon. Cigarettes will firm immediately. Cool on a wire rack until crisp. Store in an airtight cake container up to 1 week.

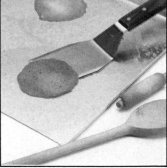

Makes 32 biscuits.

Orange Buttons

60g (2 oz/½ cup) blanched almonds, finely chopped
60g (2 oz/½ cup) mixed citrus peel, finely chopped
45g (1½ oz/⅓ cup) plain flour
60g (2 oz/¼ cup) butter, cubed
60g (2 oz/¼ cup) caster sugar

Preheat oven to 180C (350F/Gas 4). Grease a baking sheet. In a medium bowl, mix almonds and peel. Add flour. In another bowl, cream butter with sugar until fluffy. Mix almond mixture into sugar mixture; blend well. Drop by teaspoonfuls on prepared baking sheet.

Flatten gently with a fork. Bake in preheated oven 8 to 10 minutes or until biscuits are light golden brown and just set.

Cool on baking sheet on a wire rack 2 minutes. Remove from baking sheet. Cool completely on wire rack. Store in an airtight container.

Makes 40 biscuits.

Butter Fingers

30g (1 oz) butter, cubed
1½ tablespoons caster sugar
2 teaspoons cream
1 egg yolk
60g (2 oz/½ cup) plain flour
¼ teaspoon baking powder
few drops vanilla essence

TO FINISH: 45g (1½ oz) plain (dark) or milk
chocolate, chopped

Preheat oven to 170C (325F/Gas 3). Grease a
baking sheet. In a medium mixing bowl,
cream butter and sugar until fluffy; add
cream. Mix in egg yolk. Sift in flour with
baking powder; add vanilla. Mix well.

Spoon mixture into a pastry bag fitted with a
large fluted nozzle. Pipe 40 strips onto
prepared baking sheet. Bake in preheated
oven 15 to 20 minutes or until light golden
brown and firmly set. Cool on baking sheet
on wire rack 1 minute. Remove biscuit from
baking sheet; cool on wire racks.

Melt chocolate in a bowl or top of a double
boiler set over a pan of simmering water. Stir
until smooth. Dip both ends of each biscuit
into chocolate. Let stand on wire rack until
set. Store in an airtight container up to 10
days.

Makes 40 biscuits.

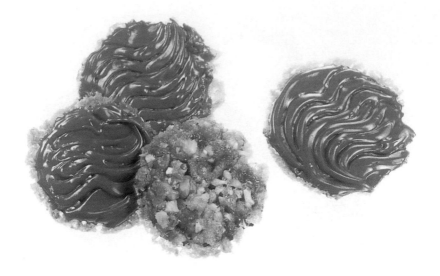

Florentines

1 tablespoon finely chopped blanched almonds
1 tablespoon finely chopped walnuts
1 tablespoon finely chopped glacé cherries
1½ tablespoons chopped mixed citrus peel
4 tablespoons brown sugar
2 tablespoons plain flour
45g (1½ oz) butter or cubed
90g (3 oz) plain (dark) chocolate, chopped

Preheat oven to 180C (350F/Gas 4). Grease 2 baking sheets. In a medium bowl, mix almonds, walnuts, cherries and citrus peel. In a small bowl, mix sugar with flour. With a pastry blender or 2 knives cut in butter until mixture resembles coarse crumbs. Add sugar mixture to fruit; mix well. Drop teaspoonsfuls of mixture about 2½ inches apart on prepared baking sheets. Flatten top of each Florentine.

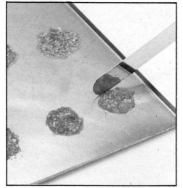

Bake in preheated oven 8 minutes or until golden. Use a palette knife to create rounds. Cool on baking sheets on wire racks until firm. Remove Florentines from baking sheets; cool completely on wire racks.

Melt chocolate in a bowl or top of a double boiler set over a pan of simmering water. Stir until smooth. Spread chocolate over flat side of Florentines, making wavy lines in chocolate with a fork. Let stand until chocolate is set. Refrigerate in an airtight container up to 1 month.

Makes 25 Florentines.

Chocolate Butter Crisps

60g (2 oz/½ cup) plain flour
60g (2 oz/½ cup) self-raising flour
pinch of salt
2 tablespoons cocoa
125g (4 oz/½ cup) butter
90g (3 oz/½ cup) icing sugar
extra icing sugar

In a medium bowl, sift flours with salt and cocoa. In another bowl, cream butter and sugar until light. Add sifted, dry ingredients; mix well. Chill 20 minutes.

Preheat oven to 180C (350F/Gas 4). Grease a baking sheet. Form mixture into 60 small balls about size of cherry. Place on prepared baking sheet.

Press with a fork dipped in icing sugar. Bake in preheated oven 8 to 10 minutes. Remove from baking sheet; cool on a wire rack. Store in an airtight tin up to 2 weeks.

Makes 60 biscuits.

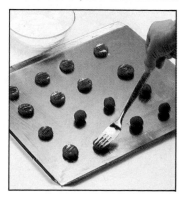

Lattice Jam Biscuits

185g (6 oz/1½ cups) plain flour
½ teaspoon baking powder
pinch of salt
125g (4 oz/½ cup) butter, cubed
125g (4 oz/½ cup) caster sugar
1 egg yolk
few drops vanilla essence
155g (5 oz/½ cup) raspberry or apricot jam

Grease baking sheet. In a medium bowl, sift flour with baking powder and salt. Tip the flour mixture into a food processor or use 2 knives, cut in butter until mixture resembles coarse crumbs. Add sugar, egg yolk and vanilla. Mix to a paste. Knead in bowl 5 seconds until mixture holds together. Divide pastry; wrap each ½ in plastic wrap. Chill for 1 hour or until firm.

On a flat surface, roll 1 section of biscuit pastry to 40 x 20cm (16 x 8in). Place on prepared baking sheet. Spread top with jam. Roll out remaining section of pastry; cut into strips. Criss-cross strips over jam to form a lattice. Chill 20 minutes.

Preheat oven to 180C (350F/Gas 4). Bake in preheated oven 25 minutes or until golden. Loosen biscuit from baking sheet. Cool completely on a wire rack. Cut biscuit into 50 pieces. Store in an airtight container up to 10 days.

Makes 50 pieces.

Almond Biscuits

1 egg
185g (6 oz/1 cup) icing sugar
grated peel of 1 lemon
few drops vanilla essence
185g (6 oz/1²/₃ cups) ground almonds
1 teaspoon baking powder

TO DECORATE: almond slivers

Line 2 baking sheets with baking paper. In a
medium bowl, beat egg with sugar 3
minutes. Add lemon peel and vanilla. Mix
in ground almonds and baking powder; stir
well.

Dampen plastic wrap. Place mixture on
plastic wrap. Form into a 40cm (16in) roll.
Freeze 1 hour.

Preheat oven to 180C (350F/Gas 4). Cut
mixture into thin slices. Space on lined
baking sheets. Return mixture to freezer.
Decorate slices with almond slivers. Bake in
a preheated oven 15 minutes or until
golden. Cool on baking sheets on wire racks
2 minutes or until crisp. Peel off paper; cool
on wire racks. Repeat procedure with
remaining mixture. Store in an airtight
container up to 2 weeks.

Makes 100 biscuits.

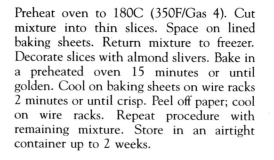

Pistachio Wafers

60g (2 oz/¼ cup) butter, cubed
60g (2 oz/¼ cup) caster sugar
few drops vanilla essence
2 egg whites
60g (2 oz/½ cup) plain flour
30g (1 oz/¼ cup) pistachio nuts

In a medium bowl, cream butter and sugar until light and fluffy. Add vanilla. In a small bowl, beat egg whites until frothy. Using whisk, gradually add egg whites to sugar mixture. Sift in ⅓ flour; stir well. Repeat twice with remaining flour. Let stand 10 minutes. In a small bowl, cover nuts with boiling water. Let stand until water is tepid. Remove skins; chop nuts finely.

Preheat oven to 180C (350F/Gas 4). Grease 2 baking sheets. Drop teaspoonfuls of wafer mixture about 3½ inches apart on prepared baking sheets. Using a knife, spread wafers to a thin circle 3 inches in diameter. Sprinkle nuts on top.

Bake in preheated oven 10 minutes or until wafers are pale brown. Remove wafers; place over a rolling pin to curve slightly. Cool on a wire rack. Repeat procedure with remaining mixture. Store in an airtight container up to 2 weeks.

Makes 30 wafers.

Coconut Fruit Strips

125g (4 oz) plain (dark) chocolate, chopped
90g (3 oz/⅓ cup) butter, melted, cooled
2 eggs, lightly beaten
185g (6 oz/1 cup) caster sugar
185g (6 oz/2 cups) dessicated coconut
4 tablespoons finely chopped glacé ginger, cherries
   or apricots

Line a swiss roll tin with foil; grease foil.
Melt chocolate in a bowl or top of a double
boiler set over a pan of simmering water. Stir
until smooth. Pour chocolate into pan;
smooth out with metal spatula to form a
smooth, thin layer. Chill 20 minutes or until
firm.

Preheat oven to 180C (350F/Gas 4). Add
butter gradually to eggs, mixing well. Stir in
sugar and coconut. Add fruit pieces. Beat for
10 seconds. Spoon mixture over chocolate
base and spread evenly.

Bake in preheated oven 25 minutes or until
top is golden brown and firm to touch.
Remove and cool 4 hours or until chocolate
base is set. Remove from pan. Invert and
peel off foil. Invert again and cut into small
squares. Store in an airtight container up to
1 week.

Makes 60 pieces.

Rocky Road Biscuits

BISCUIT CRUST: 125g (4 oz/1 cup) plain flour
pinch of salt
90g (3 oz/⅓ cup) butter, chopped
2 tablespoons icing sugar
1 egg yolk

TOPPING: 1 tablespoon thick cream
200g (6½ oz/1¼ cups) marshmallows
75g (2½ oz/½ cup) chopped, dry-roasted, unsalted
    peanuts
2 tablespoons glacé cherries, coarsely chopped

CHOCOLATE COATING: 90g (3 oz) plain (dark)
    chocolate, chopped
30g (1 oz) butter

Grease a 25 x 25cm (10 x 10in) baking pan.
In a medium bowl, sift flour and salt. With a
pastry blender or 2 knives, cut in butter until
mixture resembles coarse crumbs. Add sugar
and egg yolk. Mix well. Roll pastry between
greaseproof paper. Press to fit prepared pan
in an even layer. Prick top and chill for 20
minutes. Preheat oven to 180C (350F/Gas 4).
Bake 15 to 20 minutes or until a light golden
colour. Remove and cool on a wire rack.

To make topping, heat cream in a small
saucepan. Add marshmallows and melt over
low heat. Add nuts and cherries. Smooth
marshmallow mixture evenly over biscuit
crust. Let set.

Melt butter and chocolate in a bowl or top of
a double boiler set over a pan of simmering
water. Stir occasionally. Spread chocolate
over marshmallow. Make fork marks on the
top in a decorative pattern. Let set. Wrap
and store up to 1 week in the refrigerator. To
serve, cut pieces as needed.

Makes about 45 pieces.

Chocolate Cinnamon Wafers

45g (1½ oz/¼ cup) light brown sugar
60g (2 oz/¼ cup) caster sugar
3 egg whites
1 tablespoon and 2 teaspoons plain flour
1 tablespoon and 2 teaspoons cocoa
pinch of salt
½ teaspoon cinnamon
2 tablespoons thick cream
30g (1 oz) butter, melted

Preheat oven to 180C (350F/Gas 4). Grease and flour 2 baking sheets. Shake out excess flour. In a medium bowl, combine sugars and egg whites; whisk. Sift flour, cocoa, salt, and cinnamon into sugar mixture. Add cream and butter; mix well.

Drop 2 teaspoons of mixture on prepared baking sheets. Using a knife, spread to make a thin even circle about 10cm (4in) in diameter. Repeat procedure; each baking sheet will hold 4 wafers. Bake in a preheated oven 8 minutes. Test by lightly touching wafer. No imprint should remain if the wafer is cooked.

Remove wafers from baking sheets. Place over a rolling pin, pressing gently to curve. When crisp, cool on a rack. Repeat procedure with remaining mixture. Store within 1 hour in an airtight container up to 10 days.

Makes 30 wafers.

Brandy Snaps

90g (3 oz/⅓ cup) butter, cubed
3 tablespoons golden syrup
60g (2 oz/⅓ cup) firmly-packed light brown sugar
½ teaspoon grated fresh ginger
1 teaspoon ground ginger
60g (2 oz/½ cup) plain flour

Preheat oven to 180C (350F/Gas 4). Grease a baking sheet. In a small saucepan, cook butter, golden syrup and brown sugar over low heat until butter melts. Stir occasionally. Add fresh and ground ginger. Remove from heat. Sift flour into a medium bowl. Mix liquid into flour; stir well.

Drop a teaspoonful of mixture about 2 inches apart on prepared baking sheet. Bake in preheated oven 5 to 7 minutes or until golden brown.

Loosen brandy snaps with a spatula. Cool 5 seconds. Roll each snap smooth side outwards around handle of a wooden spoon. Cool completely on a wire rack. Repeat with remaining snaps. Store in an airtight container up to 10 days. To serve, fill with whipped cream or Orange Cream filling, page 90.

Makes 30 brandy snaps.

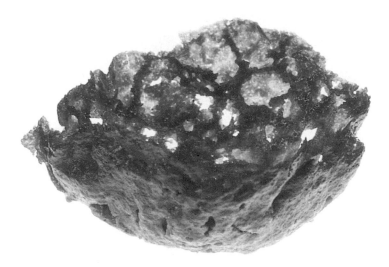

Brandy Snap Baskets

90g (3 oz/⅓ cup) butter, cubed
3 tablespoons golden syrup
60g (2 oz/⅓ cup) firmly-packed light brown sugar
½ teaspoon grated fresh ginger
1 teaspoon ground ginger
60g (2 oz/½ cup) plain flour

Preheat oven to 180C (350F/Gas 4). Grease a baking sheet. In a small saucepan, cook butter with golden syrup and brown sugar over low heat until butter melts. Stir occasionally. Add fresh and ground ginger. Remove from heat. Sift flour into a medium bowl. Mix liquid into flour; stir well.

Drop a teaspoonful of mixture about 5cm (2in) apart on prepared baking sheet. Bake in preheated oven 5 to 7 minutes or until golden brown.

To make a basket, remove 1 biscuit from sheet and place over a tiny inverted coffee cup, measuring cup or egg cup 2 seconds. Gently squeeze sides into shape. Cool on a wire rack. Repeat with remaining biscuits. Store in an airtight container up to 10 days. To serve, fill with whipped cream or Orange Cream filling, page 90, and fresh fruit.

Makes 30 baskets.

Orange Cream Filling

250 ml (8 fl oz/1 cup) thick cream
grated peel of 1 medium orange
2 tablespoons icing sugar
1 tablespoon orange liqueur

TO DECORATE: fresh strawberries or raspberries

In a small bowl, whip cream until soft peaks form. Add orange peel. Sift sugar over top. Mix well; add liqueur. Chill 2 hours.

Spoon filling into a pastry bag fitted with an open star tip. If using filling for brandy snaps, pipe a small amount of filling into each end.

If filling baskets, pipe a small amount of filling in centre. To decorate, halve strawberries; remove green hull. Place ½ a strawberry in a basket. If using raspberries, place a raspberry, and a tiny piece of mint leaf in centre of each basket. Serve immediately.

Fills 30 brandy snaps.

Chocolate Almond Crisps

185g (6 oz/1½ cup) ground almonds
100g (3½ oz/½ cup) caster sugar
pinch of salt
60g (2 oz) plain (dark) chocolate, chopped
3 egg whites
few drops vanilla essence

Preheat oven to 160C (325F/Gas 3). Line a baking sheet with baking paper. Toast almonds in a dry frying pan until golden brown. Stir occasionally. Remove pan from heat. Stir in sugar and salt.

Melt chocolate in a bowl or top of a double boiler set over a pan of simmering water. Stir until smooth. In a medium bowl, stir chocolate into almond mixture. Add 2 egg whites to form a paste. Add vanilla. In a small bowl, beat remaining egg white until stiff. Fold through mixture, ⅓ at a time.

Drop teaspoonfuls of mixture 1 inch apart on lined baking sheets. Bake in preheated oven 25 to 30 minutes or until set. Cool on baking sheet on a wire rack 5 minutes. Remove from baking sheet; cool on wire rack. Store in an airtight container up to 2 weeks.

Makes 60 biscuits.

Butter Pastry Tart Cases

125g (4 oz/1 cup) flour
pinch of salt
90g (3 oz/⅓ cup) butter, cubed
2 teaspoons icing sugar
1 tablespoon lemon juice

In a medium bowl, sift flour with salt. Place butter in centre of flour. Add sugar and lemon juice. Stir with end of a blunt knife to make a soft lumpy dough. Do not use a fork or dough will not be right consistency. Knead in bowl 8 to 10 strokes or until dough binds together. Form pastry into a ball. Wrap in plastic wrap: refrigerate 20 minutes until firm or freeze.

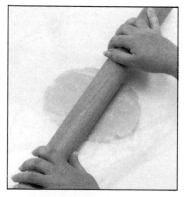

Preheat oven to 180C (350F/Gas 4). Grease 48 minature tart pans. Roll ½ of pastry very thinly between 2 layers of greaseproof paper. Using a tart pan as a cutter, press into pastry. Line tart pan with pastry circle. Repeat procedure for remaining tart pans. Refrigerate 20 minutes or until firm.

Prick pastry with skewer. Line pastry with foil. Arrange tart cases on baking sheets. Bake in preheated oven 8 to 10 minutes or until set. Remove foil. Bake 3 minutes until light golden brown. To fill, see pages 97, 99, 100.

Makes 48 tart cases.

Miniature Tarts

125g (4 oz/1 cup) plain flour
pinch of salt
30g (1 oz/¼ cup) ground almonds
100g (3½ oz/⅓ cup) butter, cubed
60 g (2 oz/⅓ cup) icing sugar
1 egg yolk
few drops vanilla essence

On a flat surface, sift flour and salt. Sprinkle ground almonds on top. Make an indentation in centre. Place butter, sugar, egg yolk and vanilla in indentation. Using fingers, work butter, sugar and egg yolk with vanilla. When partly blended, work in flour gradually from outside edges to form a paste. Knead gently 1 minute. Shape pastry into a flattened ball. Wrap in greaseproof paper; chill 2 hours. To freeze wrap in plastic wrap, or thaw in refrigerator before using.

Preheat oven to 170C (325F/Gas 3). Grease 3 baking sheets. Unwrap pastry and divide in ½. Roll to a thin layer between 2 sheets of greaseproof paper. Cut pastry into 20 rounds with a floured 2.5cm (1in) cutter. Arrange circles on prepared baking sheets. Repeat procedure with remaining ½ of pastry.

With remaining pastry, form a thin strip shaped like a sausage. Place around pastry circle to form a ridge. Prick base with a fork. Repeat procedure for each tart. Bake in preheated oven 15 to 18 minutes or until golden. Cool on baking sheets or wire racks 2 minutes. Remove from baking sheets; cool on wire racks. Store up to 1 month. To crisp, bake at 180C (350F/Gas 4) 2 minutes. To fill, see pages 94, 95, 96.

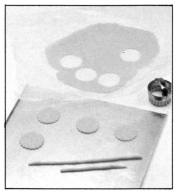

Makes 40 tarts.

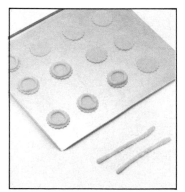

Cream Cheese Tarts

18 miniature tarts, see page 93

FILLING: 60g (2 oz/¼ cup) cream cheese
½ teaspoon grated orange peel
1 tablespoon icing sugar

TOPPING: 9 large strawberries, 36 raspberries or
    2 kiwi fruit, sliced
2 tablespoons redcurrant jelly or apricot jam

To make filling, cream cheese with orange peel and sugar in a small bowl until soft.

Place about ½ teaspoon of filling in centre of each tart case. Refrigerate up to 8 hours. Before serving, arrange fruit and jam or jelly on top. If using strawberries, cut in ½. Leave a piece of green stem on each ½. Place ½ a strawberry or a few raspberries on top of each tart. Or top each tart with a slice of kiwi fruit.

If using berries, melt redcurrant jelly in a small saucepan until thin. Use apricot jam with kiwi fruit. Using a small pastry brush, dab jelly or jam on fruit. Chill before serving.

Makes 18 tarts.

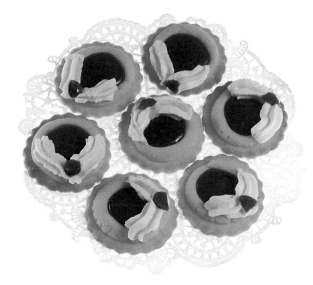

Chocolate Liqueur Tarts

24 miniature tarts, see page 93

CHOCOLATE FILLING: 300g (9½ oz) milk chocolate
1 tablespoon liquid glucose
125ml (4 fl oz/½ cup) thick cream
2 tablespoons orange liqueur, cognac or whisky

TO DECORATE: whipped cream
crystallized violet

Grate or chop chocolate.

In a small saucepan, bring glucose and cream to a boil. Add chocolate; and remove from heat. Let stand for 2 minutes. Stir until chocolate melts. Add liqueur, cognac or whisky. Stir well; cool.

Refrigerate in a covered container up to 6 weeks. Warm slightly before filling tarts. Leave to set before serving. Decorate each tart with whipped cream and small piece of crystallized violet. Serve within 4 hours.

Makes 24 tarts.

Lemon Butter Tarts

12 miniature tarts, see page 93

LEMON BUTTER FILLING: 2 eggs
220g (7 oz/1 cup) caster sugar
grated peel of 2 medium lemons
125g (4 fl oz/½ cup) lemon juice
45g (1½ oz) unsalted butter, cubed

TO DECORATE: mixed citrus peel
mint leaves

In a bowl or top of a double boiler, beat eggs
and sugar until fluffy.

Add lemon peel, lemon juice and butter.
Place a bowl on top of double boiler over a
pan of boiling water and cook, stirring until
thick. Cool; stir occasionally. Refrigerate in
a dry, sterilized container up to 4 weeks.
Makes 500 ml (16 fl oz/2 cups) mixture.

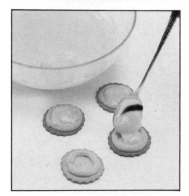

To serve, use a spoon to fill each tart with
lemon butter mixture. Decorate each tart
with a small piece of citrus peel and a mint
leaf. Store remaining filling in container in
refrigerator and use as required.

Makes 12 tarts.

Citrus Soufflé Tarts

30 butter pastry tart cases, see page 92

CITRUS SOUFFLÉ: 1 egg yolk
2 tablespoons caster sugar
grated peel of 1 medium orange
1 tablespoon lemon juice
1 teaspoon cornflour
2 tablespoons orange juice
1 large egg white
1 tablespoon sugar

Preheat oven to 180C (350F/Gas 4). In a small saucepan, whisk egg yolk, sugar, orange peel and lemon juice. In a small bowl, mix cornflour with 1 tablespoon orange juice. Add remaining orange juice; and stir into egg yolk mixture. Whisk gently over high heat to thicken evenly. Do not boil. Pour into a small bowl; cool.

In a small bowl, beat egg white until stiff. Add sugar; beat until stiff and glossy. Fold egg white into citrus mixture, ½ at a time.

Using a teaspoon form a mound of filling in each tart case; smooth top. Arrange tarts on baking sheet. Bake in preheated oven 10 minutes or until firm and light golden brown. Cool on baking sheet on wire rack 5 minutes. Remove from tart pans carefully while still warm. Cool on a wire rack. Store uncovered up to 36 hours.

Makes 30 tarts.

Miniature Swiss Tarts

125g (4 oz/¾ cup) plain flour
pinch of salt
125g (4 oz/½ cup) butter
30g (1 oz) caster sugar
few drops vanilla essence

TO FINISH: redcurrant jelly
icing sugar

Preheat oven to 180C (350F/Gas 4). Grease a baking sheet. In a small bowl, sift flour and salt. In a medium bowl, cream butter with sugar until light and fluffy. Add vanilla. Add flour mixture ½ at a time. Beat mixture 2 minutes or until soft.

Spoon mixture into a pastry bag fitted with a fluted nozzle. Pipe small rings, leaving indentation in centres, into paper cases set on a baking sheet. Bake in preheated oven 12 to 15 minutes or until light golden brown. Cool on baking sheet on a wire rack.

Fill tart cavity with redcurrant jelly. Sift sugar lightly over tarts. Store in an airtight container in a single layer up to 10 days.

Makes 60 tarts.

Almond Tarts

24 butter pastry tart cases, see page 92, warmed

ALMOND FILLING: 30g (1 oz/¼ cup) butter, cubed
30g (1 oz) caster sugar
30g (1 oz/¼ cup) ground almonds
few drops almond essence
1 egg yolk
1 teaspoon thick cream
1 teaspoon brandy

90g (3 oz/¼ cup) apricot jam
1 teaspoon lemon juice
24 slivered almonds

Preheat oven to 180C (350F/Gas 4). With a fork, cream butter. Add sugar; mix until light and fluffy. Add almonds, almond essence, egg yolk, cream, and brandy. Mix thoroughly.

In a small saucepan, warm jam and lemon juice. If lumpy, sieve or chop apricot pieces finely. Arrange tart cases on a baking sheet. Place a small dab of apricot jam in each tart cup.

Fill each tart case with almond filling. Top with an almond sliver. Bake in preheated oven 10 minutes or until set. Cool on baking sheet on a wire rack 1 minute. Run a knife around each tart edge. Cool on a wire rack. The rich flavour of these tarts will mature if they are kept for 12 hours before serving. Store up to 2 days.

Makes 24 tarts.

Chocolate Almond Tarts

25 butter pastry tart cases, see page 92

CHOCOLATE ALMOND FILLING: 1 egg
90g (3 oz/½ cup) caster sugar
2 tablespoons cocoa
60g (2 oz/½ cup) ground almonds
3 tablespoons thick cream

TO DECORATE: flaked almonds

To make filling, whisk egg and sugar until warm and lightly thickened in a bowl set over a pan of warm water. Remove bowl from pan.

Add cocoa, almonds and cream. Mix well; cool. Refrigerate up to 24 hours.

Preheat oven to 180C (350F/gas 4). Arrange tart cases on a baking sheet. Fill tart cases with filling. Decorate with almond flakes. Bake in preheated oven 8 to 10 minutes or until puffed on top and firm to touch. Cool on baking sheet on wire rack 1 minute. Remove from sheet and cool on a wire rack. Serve within 36 hours.

Makes 25 tarts.

Choux Pastry Puffs

60g (2 oz/½ cup) flour
pinch of salt
125 ml (4 fl oz/½ cup) cold water
60g (2 oz/¼ cup) butter, cubed
3 eggs

Preheat oven to 220C (425F/Gas 7). Grease and lightly flour 2 baking sheets. Shake off excess flour. Sift flour and salt onto a piece of greaseproof paper. In a small saucepan bring butter and water to boil over low heat. Butter should melt by time liquid bubbles. Remove from heat. Using greaseproof paper as a chute, add flour. Stir immediately with a wooden spoon. Mixture will thicken and form a ball in pan. Transfer to a medium bowl.

In a small bowl, beat 3 eggs with a wooden spoon. Gradually add eggs, beating well between each addition, until glossy.

To make puffs, spoon mixture into a pastry bag fitted with a plain nozzle 1cm (½in) in diameter. Pipe 50 puffs 2.5cm (1in) in diameter onto prepared baking sheets. Release pressure before lifting bag. If making éclairs, pipe 4cm (1½in) lengths. Using a pastry brush, glaze top of each puff with remaining egg. Bake in preheated oven 12 minutes. Adjust temperature to 180C (350F/ Gas 4); bake 10 minutes until the puffs are firm to touch and golden brown. Remove puffs from baking sheets. Pierce side of each puff with a small sharp knife. Turn off oven; open door. Place puffs in oven 10 minutes to dry completely; cool. Refrigerate in covered container up to 1 week or freeze wrapped up to 1 month. Crisp by baking at 180C (350F/ Gas 4) 5 minutes. To serve, see pages 102, 103, 104, 105.
Makes 50 puffs.

Coffee Cream Puffs

18 choux pastry puffs, see page 101

FILLING: 250 ml (8 fl oz/1 cup) milk
1 egg
1 tablespoon plain flour
1 tablespoon cornflour
2 tablespoons sugar
few drops vanilla essence
2 teaspoons brandy or cognac
1 teaspoon instant coffee powder
1 teaspoon hot water
2 tablespoons thick cream, whipped

ICING: 1 tablespoon cream
1 teaspoon instant coffee powder
90g (3 oz/½ cup) icing sugar

In a small saucepan, heat milk until almost boiling. In a medium bowl, beat egg with flour, cornflour and sugar. Gradually whisk milk into egg mixture. Return mixture to pan. Cook, stirring constantly 2 minutes or until mixture thickens and comes to a boil. Remove from heat; add vanilla and brandy or cognac. In a small bowl, dissolve coffee powder in hot water. Mix into hot mixture. Cool until firm. Fold in cream. Chill until thick. Filling can be frozen up to 1 month. Thaw at room temperature; stir to smooth.

Cut a small slit in side of each puff. Spoon filling into a pastry bag fitted with a plain nozzle. Fill each puff through slit. Or cut each puff in ½. Spoon filling onto bottom; replace top.

Heat cream and coffee powder until bubbling. Remove from heat. Add sugar; stir until smooth. Cook until tepid. Pour or spoon icing on top of each filled puff. Refrigerate. Eat within a few hours.

Makes 18 puffs.

Caramel Puffs

18 choux pastry puffs, see page 101
1 recipe of filling without instant coffee powder,
   see page 102

CARAMEL TOPPING: 125g (4 oz/1 cup) sugar
4 tablespoons water

Stir filling until smooth. Cut each puff in ½;
spoon filling onto bottom; replace top. Or
cut a small slit in side of each puff. Spoon
filling into a pastry bag fitted with a plain
nozzle. Fill each puff.

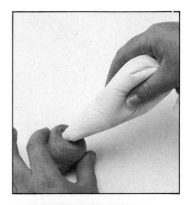

Grease a wire rack and baking sheet. Place
wire rack over baking sheet. Arrange puffs
on wire rack. To make topping, in a small
saucepan, cook sugar and water over low
heat. Shake pan occasionally until sugar
dissolves. Adjust heat to medium. Cook
rapidly until mixture is a light golden brown.
Using a pastry brush dipped in cold water,
remove sugar crystals from sides of pan.

Using a long-handled spoon, coat top of
each puff with topping. Repeat process if top
is not well covered. Let stand 10 minutes or
until caramel is firm. Using a small knife,
remove puffs from wire rack. Refrigerate up
to 12 hours.

Makes 18 puffs.

Eclairs

18 éclairs, made from choux pastry, see page 101

FILLING: 125ml (4 fl oz/½ cup) thick cream,
  whipped
few drops vanilla essence

ICING: 15g (½ oz) butter
30g (1 oz) plain (dark) chocolate, chopped
1 tablespoon cream
90g (3 oz/½ cup) icing sugar
warm water

In a small bowl, mix cream and vanilla.

Cut a small slit in one end of each éclair.
Spoon cream into a pastry bag fitted with a
plain nozzle. Fill each éclair with cream. Or
cut each éclair in ½. Spoon or pipe cream
onto bottom; replace top.

To make icing, in a small saucepan, combine
butter, chocolate and cream. Cook over low
heat until chocolate melts. Add sugar; mix
well. Stir in a small amount of warm water
until icing is smooth. Coat tops of éclairs
with chocolate icing. Serve immediately.

Makes 18 éclairs.

Praline & Orange Puffs

18 choux pastry puffs baked with topping of
  finely-chopped almonds, see page 101

FILLING: 125ml (4 fl oz/½ cup) thick cream,
  whipped
1 tablespoon icing sugar
few drops vanilla essence
grated peel of an orange
2 tablespoons finely crushed almond praline, page 29

TO FINISH: icing sugar

In a small bowl, mix cream, sugar, vanilla
and orange peel. Stir in praline, evenly.

Cut each puff ⅔ from bottom leaving ⅓ for
a cap. Spoon filling into each puff and
replace lid.

To coat, sift sugar over puffs and chill 1 hour
before serving. Refrigerate up to 12 hours.

Makes 18 puffs.

Meringue Crunchies

1 egg white
pinch of salt
90g (3 oz/⅓ cup) sugar
30g (1 oz/¾ cup) crushed cornflakes
60g (2 oz) plain (dark) chocolate, grated

Preheat oven to 170C (325F/Gas 3). In a small mixing bowl, beat egg white with salt until stiff. Gradually add sugar and beat to a stiff meringue.

In a separate bowl, mix cornflakes and chocolate. Fold into meringue.

Drop teaspoonfuls of mixture on greased baking sheet. Bake in preheated oven 20 minutes or until firm to touch. Remove from baking sheet; cool completely on a wire rack. Store in an airtight container up to 3 weeks.

Makes 50 crunchies.

Surprise Meringues

60g (2 oz/⅓ cup) dates, stoned, finely chopped
grated peel of ½ orange
2 teaspoons chopped mixed citrus peel
2 tablespoons finely chopped pecans
1 tablespoon orange juice
2 teaspoons orange liqueur
1 egg white
2 tablespoons caster sugar

In a small saucepan, cook dates, orange peel, mixed citrus peel, nuts, orange juice and liqueur. Cook over low heat for 2 minutes or until mixture is hot and dates have softened slightly. Remove from heat and cool. Form mixture into 12 small balls. Let dry for 2 hours.

Preheat oven to 170C (325F/Gas 3). Grease a baking sheet. In a small mixing bowl, beat egg white until stiff. Add sugar and beat until a stiff meringue is formed. Using a cocktail stick, dip balls into meringue, one at a time, evenly coating. Space meringues on baking sheet. Remove cocktail stick, using a second stick as a lever.

Bake in preheated oven 25 minutes or until golden and firm to touch. Remove from baking sheet; cool completely on wire rack. Serve within 6 hours, or the meringues will soften. However, if left for 24 hours they will dry again.

Makes 12 meringues.

Mushroom Meringues

2 egg whites
pinch of salt
¼ teaspoon cream of tartar
60g (2 oz/¼ cup) caster sugar
few drops vanilla essence
cocoa, sifted

FILLING: 125 ml (4 fl oz/½ cup) cream
30g (1 oz) milk chocolate, chopped
2 teaspoons brandy

Preheat oven to 150C (300F/Gas 2). Line 2 baking sheets with baking paper. In a small mixing bowl, beat egg whites with salt and cream of tartar until stiff. Gradually add sugar and vanilla and beat to a very stiff meringue. To form caps, spoon ⅔ meringue into a pastry bag fitted with a plain nozzle. Pipe 40 small mounds onto paper-lined baking sheet. Dust tops with cocoa.

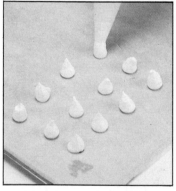

Spoon remaining meringue into a pastry bag fitted with a plain nozzle. Pipe 40 mushroom stalks on second paper-lined baking sheet. Bake meringues in preheated oven 10 minutes. Adjust oven temperature to 130C (250F/Gas ½). Bake stalks 1–1½ hours, caps 1½–2 hours until very crisp. Cool on baking sheets on wire racks. Remove cooled meringues from paper. Store in an airtight container.

To make filling, warm cream in a small saucepan. Add chocolate to cream; stir until melted. Add brandy; cool mixture before refrigerating. When mixture is completely cold, whisk gently until soft peaks form. Place filling in bottom of each meringue cap and insert a stalk. Serve immediately.

Makes 40 mushrooms.

Coffee Meringues

2 egg whites
125g (4 oz/½ cup) icing sugar
2 teaspoons instant coffee powder
2 teaspoons hot water

FILLING: 75 ml (2½ fl oz/⅓ cup) whipped cream

TO DECORATE: 16 small pieces glacé cherry

Preheat oven to 150C (300F/Gas 4). Line a baking sheet with baking paper. Beat egg whites and sugar in a bowl over a pan of simmering water until stiff. Dissolve coffee in water. Add coffee to meringue and beat. Remove ¼ cup of meringue; cover and refrigerate for use as filling.

Drop teaspoonfuls of meringue into 32 small mounds of similar size on paper-lined baking sheet. Bake meringues in preheated oven 30 minutes or until crisp. Cool on baking sheet or wire rack. Carefully remove cooled meringues from paper. Store in an airtight container up to 2 weeks.

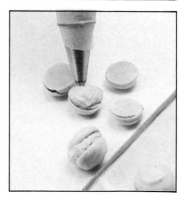

To make filling mix reserved meringue with whipped cream; blend well. Store in refrigerator up to 4 days. To serve, join pairs of meringues together with filling. Place in paper cases. To decorate, place a small piece of glacé cherry on top of cream filling.

Makes 16 petits fours.

Coconut Macaroons

125g (4 oz/¹/₂ cup) sugar
60 ml (2 fl oz/¹/₄ cup) water
2 egg whites
pinch of salt
185g (6 oz/2 cups) dessicated coconut
few drops vanilla essence

Preheat oven to 170C (325F/Gas 3). Grease 2 baking sheets. In a small saucepan, cook sugar and water until sugar dissolves. Adjust heat to medium; cook syrup to soft ball stage (115C/234F). Syrup should form a small round ball when dropped into a cup of cold water. In a medium bowl, beat egg whites and salt until stiff. Gradually add sugar syrup, beating constantly until mixture is thick and glossy.

Add coconut and vanilla. Stir well.

Drop teaspoonfuls 1 inch apart on prepared baking sheets. Use a wet spatula to even sides. Bake in preheated oven 20 to 25 minutes until crisp and light golden brown. Remove from baking sheets. Cool on a wire rack. Store in an airtight container up to 6 weeks.

Makes 50 macaroons.

Tiny Meringues

2 egg whites
pinch of salt
¼ teaspoon cream of tartar
60g (2 oz/¼ cup) caster sugar
few drops vanilla essence
FILLING: 125 ml (4 fl oz/½ cup) whipped cream
blueberries, raspberries, redcurrants or baby
    strawberries
TO DECORATE: 30 small pieces of angelica or baby
    mint leaves

Preheat oven to 150C (300F/Gas 2). Line a baking sheet with baking paper. Beat egg whites until stiff with salt and cream of tartar. Add ½ sugar and beat again. Add remainder of sugar and beat until very stiff. Add vanilla.

Form teaspoonfuls of meringue into 30 small flat buttons on paper-lined baking sheet. Spoon remaining meringue into small pastry bag fitted with a small fluted nozzle. Pipe around edge of circles, keeping well inside bottom to form a casing.

Bake meringues in preheated oven 10 minutes. Adjust oven temperature to 130C (250F/Gas ½). Bake until the meringues are crisp to touch and lightly coloured. If meringues begin to darken, turn oven off and let stand to crisp. Cool on baking sheet on wire rack. Carefully remove cooled meringues from paper. Store in an airtight tin up to 2 weeks. To fill meringues, spoon cream into a small pastry bag fitted with a fluted nozzle. Pipe a small rosette into the centre of meringue. Top with blueberries, raspberries, redcurrants or a tiny strawberry. Decorate with angelica or mint leaves. Serve immediately.

Makes 30 meringues.

Chocolate Nut Fudge

125g (4 oz/½ cup) butter, cubed
185 ml (6 fl oz/¾ cup) milk
4 tablespoons cocoa
750g (1½ lb/3⅓ cups) sugar
few drops vanilla essence
60g (2 oz/½ cup) finely chopped pecans or walnuts

Grease a 27 x 18cm (11 x 7in) baking pan. Line bottom with foil.

In a large saucepan, melt butter, add milk. Sift in cocoa; add sugar. Cook over medium heat to dissolve sugar. Shake saucepan rather than stirring mixture. Bring mixture to a boil. Cook until mixture reaches 114C (238F) or until a small piece dropped into cold water forms a soft ball.

Remove from heat. Let cool 5 minutes. Beat with a wooden spoon until thick but still glossy. Add vanilla and nuts. Pour mixture into prepared pan; press down firmly. Let cool 2 hours. To remove fudge from pan, run a knife around edge of pan and invert. Remove foil and cut into 50 pieces. Store in refrigerator in an airtight container up to 4 weeks.

Makes 50 pieces.

Festive Fudge

250 ml (8 fl oz/1 cup) milk
125g (4 oz/½ cup) butter, cubed
675g (1 lb 5 oz/3 cups) sugar
few drops vanilla essence
2 tablespoons finely chopped glacé cherries
2 tablespoons finely chopped glacé ginger
2 tablespoons finely chopped walnuts

Lightly grease an 15 x 15cm (6 x 6in) loaf pan. In a small saucepan, bring milk to boil. Add sugar and butter. Cook on low heat uncovered to 116C (240F) or until a soft ball is formed. Use a sugar thermometer to maintain an even temperature. Stir occasionally.

Remove from heat and add vanilla, cherries, ginger and nuts. For a firm grainy texture, beat immediately with a wooden spoon. For a softer texture, let cool to 50C (115F) before beating.

Pour mixture into prepared greased pan; cool before cutting. For softer fudge, leave 12 hours before cutting. Store in an airtight container up to 3 weeks.

Makes about 50 pieces.

Mocha Coconut Roughs

125g (4 oz/1⅓ cups) dessicated coconut
125g (4 oz) milk chocolate, chopped
125g (4 oz) plain (dark) chocolate, chopped
30g (1 oz) butter, melted
2 teaspoons instant coffee granules

Toast coconut in a dry frying pan. Stir until golden brown. Remove and cool.

Melt milk and plain chocolate in a bowl or top of a double boiler set over a pan of simmering water. Stir in butter, coffee and coconut.

Drop by teaspoonfuls onto non-stick baking paper to set. Store for up to 1 month.

Makes 60 pieces.

Marshmallow Chocolate Balls

45g (1½ oz/¼ cup) raisins or sultanas
1 tablespoon brandy
60g (2 oz/¼ cup) butter
90g (3 oz) plain (dark) chocolate, chopped
90g (3 oz/1 cup) dessicated coconut
155g (5 oz) marshmallows
2 teaspoons cream

Soak raisins or sultanas in brandy for 24 hours until brandy has been absorbed and raisins are plump. Melt butter in a small saucepan. Remove from heat and add chocolate. Let stand covered until chocolate has softened. Stir until smooth. Add raisins and brandy. Pour mixture into a medium bowl. Refrigerate until firm enough to form into tiny balls. Chill balls until firm.

Toast coconut in a frying pan. Stir frequently so colour is even. Spread on a plate to cool. Combine marshmallows and cream in a bowl or top of a double boiler set over a pan of simmering water. Stir until marshmallows melt. This mixture should be just warm for dipping chocolate balls.

Place a chocolate ball in a teaspoon and dip into marshmallow mixture. Lift immediately. Roll ball in coconut until coated. Marshmallow can be shaped after ball is rolled in coconut. Place on a plate. Continue until all balls are coated. Refrigerate until firm. Store covered with foil between layers in refrigerator.

Makes 24

Chocolate Torrone

60g (2 oz) plain (dark) chocolate, chopped
1 tablespoon rum
60g (2 oz/¼ cup) butter
1 tablespoon icing sugar
1 small egg yolk
30g (1 oz/¼ cup) ground almonds
1 egg white
2 tablespoons roughly broken plain sweet biscuits

Line miniature pan of 250 ml (8 fl oz/1 cup) capacity with foil and grease lightly. Place chocolate and rum in a bowl or top of a double boiler set over a pan of simmering water. Melt and stir until smooth. Let stand until tepid.

Beat butter until creamy. Stir in sugar, egg yolk and ground almonds. Beat chocolate into butter mixture a little at a time. Beat egg white until stiff; fold into chocolate mixture ⅓ at a time. Mix in biscuit pieces.

Spoon mixture in pan and smooth top. Cover with plastic wrap; chill for 6 hours or until firm. To unmould, run a knife around edge and invert Torrone. Slice into 10 pieces and then cut each slice in ½. Refrigerate until served.

Makes 20 pieces.

Chocolate Kirsch Log

125g (4 oz) plain (dark) chocolate
60g (2 oz/½ cup) finely chopped blanched almonds
1 tablespoon kirsch
60g (2 oz/⅓ cup) icing sugar
1 egg white

FILLING: 30g (1 oz) butter
1 egg yolk
1 tablespoon icing sugar
2 tablespoons cherries, finely chopped

TO DECORATE: cocoa or grated plain (dark)
   chocolate

In a medium bowl, grate chocolate and mix
with almonds. Add kirsch and sugar.
Gradually add egg white, until mixture binds
well. Form mixture into a log shape. Flatten
to 30 x 10cm (12 x 4in).

To make filling, cream butter in a small
bowl. Add egg yolk and sugar; mix well. Stir
in chopped cherries. Spread filling evenly in
a strip along log. Fold over log to enclose
filling. Chill 20 minutes.

To decorate, roll log in cocoa or grated
chocolate to coat the outside. Wrap log in
greaseproof paper and then in foil;
refrigerate. To serve, cut slices as needed and
serve them very cold. It freezes well and can
be cut frozen, then left to thaw 5 minutes.
Refrigerated it keeps well for 3 weeks,
frozen, 3 months.

Makes 30 pieces.

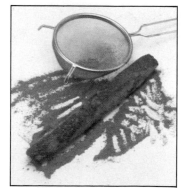

Christmas Puddings

125g (4 oz/¾ cup) finely chopped dried figs
60g (2 oz/½ cup) ground almonds
2 tablespoons icing sugar
60g (2 oz) plain (dark) chocolate, grated
2 teaspoons brandy
2 teaspoons lemon juice
1 egg white
TOPPING: 1 tablespoon cream
60g (2 oz) white chocolate
1 teaspoon brandy

TO DECORATE: marzipan, page 40, green food
colouring, 1 red glacé cherry

In a medium mixing bowl, mix figs, almonds, sugar, plain chocolate, brandy and lemon juice. Add egg white, a teaspoon at a time, to bind mixture. Mixture should be moist. Chill for 2 hours. Form a small walnut sized ball. Roll in palm of hand until smooth. Using a very sharp knife, cut off ⅓ of ball so ball will sit flat. Repeat, returning extra piece to mixture each time. Refrigerate in a covered container up to 2 weeks.

To make topping, heat cream in a small saucepan until bubbling. Remove from heat and add chocolate. Cover and let stand 5 minutes. Add brandy. Stir until smooth. Trickle topping over each pudding to simulate custard.

To decorate, add green food colouring to marzipan; knead well. Pinch off 40 tiny pieces. Roll each piece into a rectangle. To make leaves, press centre of each rectangle and flatten, leaving end as a point. Curve each leaf slightly. Let dry 2 hours. Cut glacé cherry into small pieces. Place 2 leaves on top of each pudding and piece of cherry in centre. Refrigerate in a single layer until puddings are firm, or up to 1 week.

Makes 20 puddings.

Nut Snowballs

30g (1 oz/¼ cup) finely ground almonds
30g (1 oz/¼ cup) finely ground hazelnuts
90g (3 oz/½ cup) icing sugar
1 egg white

TO COAT: 2 egg whites
icing sugar

Preheat oven to 180C (350F/Gas 4). Line bottom of baking sheet with greaseproof paper. In a small bowl, mix nuts together. Add sugar; gradually add sufficient egg white to form a paste.

Wet hands; form nut paste into 24 small round balls. In a small bowl whisk 2 egg whites lightly until slightly frothy. Dip balls into egg whites; roll in icing sugar to coat.

Place in paper cases on baking sheet and bake 12 to 15 minutes or until golden on top and firm to touch. Remove from baking sheet; cool on a wire rack 12 hours. Dust with a little extra icing sugar. Store in an airtight container up to 1 week. To serve, place in paper cases.

Makes 24 snowballs.

Glazed Hazelnut Matchsticks

30g (1 oz/¼ cup) hazelnuts
caster sugar
185g (6 oz) puff pastry

ICING: 90g (3 oz/½ cup) icing sugar
¼ teaspoon lemon juice
½ egg white

Preheat oven to 180C (350F/Gas 4). Grease hazelnuts on a baking sheet 10 minutes or until golden brown and skins are slightly blistered. Wrap nuts in a towel. Let stand 5 minutes. Rub with towel to remove skins. Finely chop nuts. To make icing, in a small bowl, mix icing sugar and lemon juice. Add egg white, gradually; beat well. Cover tightly and refrigerate 1 hour.

Grease a baking sheet. On a flat surface sprinkled with caster sugar, roll puff pastry to a very thin 28 x 18cm (11 x 7in) strip. Sprinkle pastry with ⅔ chopped nuts. Fold lengthwise into centre. Roll again to a thickness of about ½ inch. Place pastry on prepared baking sheet. Cut pastry into 3 long strips; divide strips into ½ inch pieces. Chill for 30 minutes.

Preheat oven to 220C (425F/Gas 7). Stir icing before spreading over the top of each strip. Top with remainder of nuts. Bake in preheated oven 10 minutes or until golden. Adjust oven temperature to 180C (350F/Gas 4). Bake 5 minutes or until centre of pastry is cooked. Let stand on baking sheet 1 minute. Carefully cut between strips where icing has joined matchsticks together. Loosen strips from baking sheet. Let stand until completely cold. Store matchsticks in an airtight container up to 2 weeks.
Makes about 40 matchsticks.

Marshmallow Nut Fudge

300g (10 oz) marshmallows
90g (3 oz/⅓ cup) butter, cubed
1 tablespoon water
185g (6 oz) plain (dark) chocolate, chopped
few drops vanilla essence
185g (6 oz/1¼ cups) coarsely chopped walnuts

Line bottom of 23 x 10cm (9 x 4 in) loaf pan with foil. In a medium saucepan, melt marshmallows, butter and water. Stir occasionally. Add chocolate, vanilla and nuts to marshmallow mixture. Stir until evenly mixed and chocolate has melted.

Pour into prepared pan. When cool, refrigerate wrapped in foil.

To serve, cut into 40 pieces.

Makes 40 pieces.

Twice Dipped Strawberries, page 13, make a
refreshing after dinner treat. They can also
be packed prettily and presented as a small
gift or used to decorate rich gâteaux.

A selection of Miniature Tarts: Chocolate
Liqueur Tarts, page 95; Cream Cheese Tarts,
page 94; Lemon Butter Tarts, page 96.

This attractive bunch of grapes is made from
a selection of chocolate trufflles, such as
Almond Praline Truffles, page 30; Orange
Truffles, page 33; Ginger Truffles, page 35;
Cake Truffles, page 36; Almond Prune
Truffles, page 37. Assemble truffles of varying
sizes, fix in place using a little melted
chocolate, pipe chocolate stalks and
decorate with a chocolate leaf.

Clockwise from top: Almond Biscuits, page 83; Brandy Snaps, page 88; Chocolate Almond Crisps, page 91; Orange Buttons, page 78; Viennese Almond Crescents, page 72; Almond Orange Bread, page 68; Meringue Crunchies, page 106; Chocolate Chip Bars, page 75, presented in a box tied with velvet ribbon and packed in tissue.

An assortment of wafers served with soft
fruits. Clockwise from top: Chocolate
Cinnamon Wafers, page 87; Cigarettes
Russes, page 77; Pistachio Wafers, page 84.

Clockwise from top: Fruit-Filled Chocolate
Cases, page 28; Chocolate-Coated Orange
Strips, page 12; Cherry Nut Chocolates,
page 16; Mocha Coconut Roughs, page 114;
Chocolate-Coated Fruit, page 10; Fruity
Chocolates, page 8; Marzipan Cherry Log,
page 43; Chocolate Marzipan Delights, page
42; Walnut Coffee Creams, page 17;
Chocolate-Coated Fruit, page 10, presented
as a tempting array of fruit, nut and
marzipan confections.

INDEX